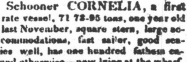

The saltworks began at the shore where windmills pumped sea water from reservoirs up to the evaporating vats to make salt. These structures dotted the landscapes near the shores of every Cape Cod town. *Photo from the H.K. Cummings Collection.*

The Saltworks of
Historic Cape Cod

A Record of the Nineteenth Century

Economic Boom in Barnstable County

By William P. Quinn

The Saltworks in South Yarmouth operated into the 1860's. This is a view of the vast acreage of the evaporators in that area. Over a period of several years, the upland beaches of the Cape were lined with hundreds of vats such as these, evaporating thousands of gallons of sea-water to make salt, and salt by-products. At the height of the salt business, companies from Provincetown to Woods Hole employed some $2 million of capital in the business. Shores were dotted with the square peaked-roof vats on stilts which must have looked like small villages and the sound of whirring mills was heard throughout the land. *Photo courtesy of Stanley Snow, Orleans, Mass.*

PREFACE

The salt industry in Barnstable County was spawned during the Revolutionary War when England blockaded our coasts and denied the colonists the basic needs of life. The practice of making salt was one of necessity here because the fishing fleet could not operate without it. After a few years of development, the manufacture of salt by solar evaporation was a catalyst for the genesis of other local industries and business expanded aggressively. The entrepreneurs on Cape Cod were among some of the major traders along the entire American east coast.

The saltworks would be an environmentalist's delight today. Nature did most of the work and there was almost no pollution resulting from the process. The wind, sun and gravity were the unpaid servants. The ingenious Cape Codders were the ones who profited and the return on invested capital was substantial. Cheaper salt sources elsewhere caused this profitable Cape industry to decline and the passage of time advanced the ultimate end to the business. But for forty years the Cape had reaped bountiful profits from the ocean by evaporating sea water and selling the remaining sodium chloride.

Throughout the nineteenth century, the sailing vessel carried most of this nation's commerce to all corners of the world. This is a painting of the hermaphrodite brig *Alice Putnam,* and was typical of the early deepwater trading ships that plied the waters around Cape Cod. *From the H.K. Cummings Collection.*

CONTENTS

Chapter One - The Genesis of the Salt Works on Cape Cod   1

Chapter Two - The Development of Solar Evaporation   15

Chapter Three - Expansion of the Salt Trade   33

Chapter Four - Salt Taxes and the Packet Boats   55

Chapter Five - The Diverse Cape Cod Industries   77

Chapter Six - The Upper Cape Towns   105

Chapter Seven - The Mid Cape Towns   119

Chapter Eight - The Outer Cape Towns   141

Chapter Nine - The Lower Cape Towns   163

Chapter Ten - The Decline of the Salt Works   179

Appendix   207

Bibliography   232

Index   234

Index of Saltworks Owners   237

List of Illustrations   241

Enoch Harding's Saltworks plans   243

The early family homestead on Cape Cod was a large double Cape with several sleeping rooms and a central fireplace in the kitchen where all the cooking was done. The house was surrounded by several sheds and a barn to shelter the livestock. The several acres around the buildings served as farmland for crops and pasture land for the animals. One important part of the farm was the root cellar. A large hole dug in the ground and lined with rocks. This room was covered with sod and the temperature inside usualy stayed at almost forty degrees year-round. It was an excellent place to keep vegetables, butter and other perishable foods. In those early days, survival meant that every home had to be self sufficient.

The Genesis of the Salt Works
on Cape Cod.

Chapter One

The history of the Cape Cod Salt Works began over two hundred years ago, when a perceptive fishing boat captain from Quivet Neck in Yarmouth, (later to become part of the town of Dennis,) began experimenting with the manufacture of salt. His ingenius device produced sodium chloride by the evaporation of sea water utilizing the warm summer sun to do most of the work. Everyday life on Cape Cod in the latter part of the 18th century was very different from what we know today. To appreciate fully the conditions under which people lived in that era, we must turn the calendar back to the days when there were no electric lights, automobiles, television sets, radios or running water. None of the everyday conveniences we take for granted today, existed. Indoor plumbing had not been invented at that time. Modern medicine was one hundred and fifty years into the future. Large families, with a dozen or more children, were reared in order to carry on the heavy work load involved in producing the basic necessities needed for all.

A stranger visiting Cape Cod in those days would find some strange looking structures throughout the countryside. The large wind mills, strategically placed on the high hills, were unique but not necessarily considered picturesque at that time. They were, however, vital for each community to grind its grain into flour. Different too were the saltworks. They were erected near the tide waters, low to the ground, each with a roof that could be moved easily on rollers. Nearby, there were small wind mills atop a framework of timbers on the beach, adjacent to the salt vats, for the purpose of pumping sea-water. They were called salt-mills. The development of the Cape Cod saltworks is a story that began during the Revolutionary War and ended nearly a hundred years later.

When the settlers first arrived in the early 17th century, houses were clustered together for protection against hostile natives. But later, after this danger passed, they were normally built a good distance from each other. The 18th century farms consisted of anywhere from fifty to one hundred acres, and many were even larger. The style of living on the Cape in those days differed greatly from what it is in modern times. When food, clothing or other necessities are needed today, we have only to get in an automobile, drive into town and purchase these items at stores. In the late 18th century, the acquisition of these articles was accomplished by a lot of hard work.

The homesteads at that time were self sufficient. No retail outlets in which to buy necessities existed. All the family's food was grown on the land. Cattle were raised for draft animals and meat. The two principal professions on Cape Cod at the beginning of the nineteenth century were farming and fishing. The more timid men stayed ashore and tilled the land while the stouthearted ones went to sea. Many of the large families had one or more members at sea fishing, because the early commerce involved either farm products or seafood. Fish was one of the major staples on the Cape in colonial times; another was corn. Clothing was made from raw materials. There was a spinning wheel in almost every home. The women of the house spent their long winter evenings spinning the linen and wool threads. The flax was grown on the farm. The women also wove the thread into cloth and sewed homespun clothing for everyone in the household. The wife had to cook, repair clothing, clean house and sometimes help in the fields with the planting or harvest. She made her own soap and tallow candles. If there were saltworks nearby, she would help there whenever an extra helping-hand was needed. Her day began before dawn and lasted until well after dark. And, in addition, she bore and reared a dozen or more children. It was probably about this time that they coined the adage: "A man may work from sun to sun but a woman's work is never done."

This is the remains of saltworks at South Yarmouth. The salt mills are on the right side of the photograph with a building for drying in the center and salt vats on the left. This was probably taken at a late date because the salt mill on the right does not have any wind vanes and the vat on the left appears to be in need of repairs. *Photo courtesy of Alec & Audrey Todd, Yarmouth, Mass.*

Salt is basic to life and references to salt in literature and folklore are abundant. The Bible has several stories. The Lord warned Lot's wife not to look back. She ignored the warning and was turned into a pillar of salt. In Matthew, (5:13), "salt of the earth" describes a man with unpretentious integrity. In the age old debate about creation and evolution, some people believe that mankind originally evolved from the sea. It is interesting to note that the chemical composition of human blood is very similar to that of sea water. There are several different everyday references to common salt. Webster's dictionary describes it as "a substance used for seasoning and preserving food from the earliest ages, its chemical name being chloride of sodium, obtained from mines or by the evaporation of sea-water." There are many uses of the term *salt*. The salt-cellar was a small glass vessel used to hold the seasoning for use at the dinner table. Commonly used in the nineteenth century, it is now a rare item. There were several different types

A pair of rare pieces in the Sandwich Glass Museum are these Lafayette salt cellars. These small seasoners were common on the dinner tables in the 19th century. *Photo by William P. Quinn.*

of salt-cellars manufactured by the Sandwich Glass Works (1826-1887) which are treasured heirlooms today. The salt-box house is so called because it was shaped similar to the saltboxes used in early kitchens, beside the hearth where the cooking was done.

A salter is a manufacturer of salt whereas a saltern is the saltworks, a structure in which salt is made by the boiling or evaporation of sea water. A salt marsh is land covered by ocean water during high course spring tides and is adjacent to salt water estuaries but more important, it is an area rich in production of nutritional algae which is distributed through the food chain of marine animals. An old salt is a veteran sailor who can spin yarns about going "round the Horn" (this, in reference to Cape Horn and the nineteenth century sailors who fought their way through the storms common to the waters around the tip of South America). There are several other references to this unique compound. We use salt on our food every day and it is widely used in the manufacture of the many different packaged foods we buy in the store. The use of rock salt is common today on highways during winter storms to melt the ice and snow.

The sprawling Boston and Sandwich Glass Works factory in Sandwich covered almost six acres. The glass produced in this plant was valued in excess of a half a million dollars each year. *Photo by H.K. Cummings.*

The local histories are replete with stories about the early Cape Cod saltworks but very little detail is included about this important business. The late 18th century area newspapers hardly mention the development except for the salt cargoes, listed in the maritime news and carried by coastal schooners. The adage "necessity is the mother of invention" is not a correct assumption. At the time, there were no important discoveries made here because this particular technology already existed in Europe. The important feature of the industry on Cape Cod was the unique vats constructed to carry out the process. There were also several original improvements applied to the evaporating structures conceived by the residents. These were necessary to facilitate the local operations. The beginning of this industry on Cape Cod resulted in a burgeoning effect for several types of small factories of various types around Barnstable County. The outcome was a diverse expansion of several businesses that grew during the saltworks period and continued after the industry's gradual demise. It was an exciting era in which to live, where ingenuity and hard work had abundant rewards.

Since time immemorial, salt (sodium chloride) has been one of man's indispensable necessities. It was used in the early days as a preservative for meat, fish, and other organic compounds that decay rapidly without refrigeration. Today, the use of salt by human beings is continually being studied by the medical profession. A popular belief has always prevailed that the regular use or an excess of salt in the diet would lead to high blood pressure. This theory has been questioned lately by researchers and no definitive result has been forthcoming. Salt has a long history through the measure of man's time on earth. The compound was once used as part of the salary for soldiers in the Roman army. It was during this time that the old saying "not worth his salt" was coined.

In 1624, a man was sent from England to begin a *"saltworks"* in Plymouth but he failed to convince the Pilgrims that he could operate a saltern. His methods were correct but the New England climate was not compatible with his efforts. His operations called for evaporation of sea water in pans dug out of the ground and lined with clay, much the same way as it was done in southern Europe. Governor Bradford lost patience with the man after a year of trials. He was sent to Cape Ann but he fared no better there and salt continued to be imported. There was some local manufacturing of salt but this was by boiling sea water in huge iron vats. The Cape Cod towns were settled in the 1640's by those early Pilgrims, who concentrated their labors on farming and livestock. A variety of endeavors soon followed. The men from Plymouth began to develop other products from their large forests: clapboards, pipestaves, hoops, and rough hewn lumber were traded across the ocean for manufactured goods not available at home. The primary export in Colonial times, however, was from the sea.

The Pilgrims were not fishermen in the beginning but the Indians taught them to gather the herring that migrated, each spring, up local brooks to spawn. The fish were used for food at home and fertilizer on their crops. The Pilgrims dug shellfish from the shore and caught eels but it was several years before there was any significant harvest of codfish. When the offshore fisheries began, they had to cope with New England's capricious weather. The conditions here were dissimilar to other parts of the country and changed frequently, sometimes without warning. Fishing later became the major economic staple in the pioneer villages.

As years passed, vast fish stocks in New England waters produced bountiful landings, far beyond the needs of local consumption. The fish were dried, salted and then stowed aboard vessels for export. The amount of salt needed for this endeavor was prodigious and local salt makers could not meet the demand. Thus, imported salt was vital to the survival of the fishing industry. Another important use for salt was in the fur trade. The native Americans traded furs for domestic goods and the furs were exported to Europe where the demand was greatest. Those exported were bear, beaver, moose and otter. It was a convenient marriage of cargo. Fish and furs could be carried, in separate holds, both well salted. Throughout this period, foreign markets for other New England products were being developed as well. Inventive Yankee ingenuity helped to make this area the workshop of the nation. This activity was well known in England and it wasn't long before the British crown decided to overtax the people in the colonies. Protests by the Colonists were ignored and an autocratic local government was seated. This only made matters worse; ultimately leading to the Revolutionary War and, later, independence for the colonies.

New England's growing maritime commerce improved measurably in the second half of the 18th century. Later, with fishing as the basic foundation of the economy, some problems developed. During this period in history, commercial ice or refrigeration did not exist. The fishermen depended on salt to preserve their catch. Some salt was imported from the Caribbean but most of it came in from southern Europe. With the outbreak of war, salt from these overseas sources was cut off by the British blockade. The people turned to boiling sea water in large iron kettles to obtain the necessary salt. This practice proved inefficient because of the enormous supply of wood needed for the fires and the quantity of salt obtained was very small. It took almost two cords of firewood to boil down four hundred gallons of sea water and produce one bushel of salt. The production realized for the amount of labor and fuel expended was inefficient. Home salt was made by boiling salt water in an iron kettle over the fire on the hearth. There was little waste there as the home fires were kept going most of the time for heating and cooking.

Other primitive works of various kinds dotted the seaside. One technique was to drive stakes into the bottom of tidal ponds. Salt was deposited on the stakes as the water evaporated but very little was obtained in this manner. The local Indians obtained their salt when sea water splashed upon hollowed rocks along the shore. The small pools evaporated in the hot sun and the white powder residue was used by the native Americans in their food. One problem with salt acquired by these methods was that it was impure. During the Revolutionary War, Congress placed a bounty on salt to stimulate its manufacture and this was the incentive for more imagination. Cape Codders had ample amounts of these qualities and it wasn't long before their imagination caught up with their incentive.

A look into the descriptions of life on Cape Cod for this period (1837) is quoted from the travels of J. W. Barber.

"Food can so easily be procured, either on the shores or in the sea, that, with the profit which arises from their voyages, in which it must be confessed they labor very hard, the people are enabled to cover their tables well with provisions. A breakfast among the inhabitants, and even among those who are called the poorest, for there are none which may be called really poor, consists of tea or coffee, brown bread, generally with butter, sometimes without, and salt or fresh fish, fried or broiled. A dinner affords one or more of the following dishes: roots and herbs; salted beef or pork boiled; fresh butcher's meat not more than twelve times a year; wild fowl frequently in the autumn and winter; fresh fish boiled or fried with pork; shellfish; salt fish boiled; Indian pudding; pork baked with beans. Tea or coffee also frequently constitutes part of the dinner. A supper consists of tea or coffee, and fish, as at breakfast; cheese, cakes made of flour, gingerbread, and pies of several sorts. This bill of fare was served, with little variation, for all the fishing towns in the county. In many families there is no difference between the breakfast and supper; cheese, cakes, and pies being common at the one as at the other."

"About Cape Cod houses: These have one story, and four rooms on the lower floor; and are covered on the sides as well as the roofs with pine shingles, eighteen inches in length. The chimney is in the middle, immediately behind the front door, and on each side of the door are two windows. The roof is straight; under it are two chambers; and there are two larger and two smaller windows in the gable end. This is the general structure and appearance of the great body of houses from Yarmouth to Race Point. There are, however, several varieties, but of too little importance to be described. A great proportion of them are in good repair. Generally they exhibit a tidy, neat aspect in themselves and in their appendages, and furnish proofs of comfortable living, by which I was at once disappointed and gratified. The barns are usually neat, but always small."

"Clams are found on many parts of the shores of New England, but nowhere in greater abundance than at Orleans. Formerly five hundred barrels were dug here for bait; but the present year 1,000 barrels have been collected. Between one and two hundred of the poorest of the inhabitants are employed in this business; and they receive from their employers three dollars a barrel for digging the clams, opening, salting them, and filling the casks. From 12 to 18 bushels of clams in the shell must be dug, to fill, when opened, a barrel. A man by this labor can earn seventy-five cents a day; and women and children are also engaged in it. A barrel of clams are worth six dollars; the employers, therefore, after deducting the expense of salt and the casks, which they supply, still obtain a handsome profit. A thousand barrels of clams are equal in value to six thousand bushels of Indian corn, and are procured with no more labor and expense. When therefore the fishes, with which the coves of Orleans abound, are also taken into consideration, they may justly be regarded as more beneficial to the inhabitants, than if the space which they occupy was covered with the most fertile soil."

The 1717 Meeting House in Barnstable where, in the 18th century, Sunday attendance was manditory for the whole town. Today it is the West Parish Congregational Church and on Sundays, most of the pews are full without any compulsary laws. *Photo by William P. Quinn.*

There were other interesting manners of living about the people of Cape Cod during the first part of the 19th century. Church was held on Sunday and everyone was required to attend. A law passed at Plymouth in 1670 insured a full congregation every Sunday. And although the penalties for missing the services were not harsh, a person sometimes had to spend a day locked in a pillory and be humiliated before his neighbors after missing a Sunday meeting. The sermons usually lasted between six and seven hours with an hour off for lunch in the middle of the day. This interval was frequently spent at the local nearby tavern. The respite provided time to warm the body, inside and out. The tavern's potent toddy helped warm the

The saltworks on Bass River at South Yarmouth. The logs in the foreground were hollowed out and used as pipes to pump water to the vats for evaporation. These appear to be crane works *Photo courtesy of Alec & Audrey Todd, Yarmouth, Mass.*

spiritual well being (and the body) in the winter, and cool the sweltering congregations in the summer. During this period in American history, there was a bracing beverage called "Flip." The recipe varied with each tavern but generally it was made in a great pewter mug. The container was two thirds full of strong beer which had been sweetened with sugar and molasses. Sometimes dried pumpkins were used. Then a liberal portion of New England rum was stirred in. It was ready after a red-hot poker was thrust into the mixture. This changed the flavor to a burnt, bitter taste but it was loved by all at that time. The imbibers must have had rugged constitutions as this drink would probably not be popular with the cocktail drinkers of today.

Food was plentiful and the people lived in comfortable Cape Cod cottages. Most everyone, including the women and children, kept busy. The saltworks ordinarily employed older men to watch over the vats and keep an eye on the young boys who played around them. It was great fun for the lads to slide down the movable roofs of the saltworks. This usually resulted in a warming of the seat of their pants - twice. Once when they slid down the roof, the second time when they came home and their Mothers saw the condition of the clothes that she had spent untold hours making. Most of the clothes worn in those days were of homespun material. The women did the work of manufacturing clothes for the entire family by spinning, weaving and sewing, from shorn wool to finished garment. Dubious explanations about ruined clothes usually resulted in a trip to the woodshed for obvious reasons. There were other amusements for mischievous boys around the saltworks. They would sometimes cut holes in the wooden pipes and create a great spurt of water under pressure. The Author, being the father of two sons, can attest to the fact that young boys have a penchant for deviltry and the lads of the early nineteenth century were probably no different at that time than they are today.

Captain Levi Crowell of Yarmouth kept a diary of his adventures* from the time he was a boy through his adult years. He described life in the middle of the nineteenth century:

"My mother had a spinning wheel and a loom. I well remember seeing her spin yarn and weave cloth, and I assisted her in making candles by pouring the hot tallow into heavy iron candle molds and letting it harden. Tallow candles and oil lamps were the only means of lighting our houses then. At first we used whale-oil lamps, which made only a pretty poor light and gave off a strong oily smell. When the coal oil came into use, it was a welcome improvement. The row of bedtime candles was still lined up on the kitchen shelf, while the cheerful oil lamp on the sitting room table was the center of family activity. Some families put up oil lamps on posts near their gates to light their dooryards but, for the most part, the streets were pitch dark at night - unless there was a full moon. My mother always kept a lamp burning in a kitchen window that overlooked the Cove when we boys went eeling at night, so that we could have a range to guide us home in the darkness."

This type of living was endured by all with an appreciation for what little they had and a determination to work for something better. If a man needed lumber to build his house or a barn, he cut the logs from the woods. He used ancient tools to mill the logs into boards, needed to build the structure. In those times, when new beams were being raised, it was often a neighborhood effort. People from all around came to help erect the building. The women cooked food and when the work was done, a large table fed the workers. Frequently it was a two or three day affair enjoyed by all. No one was paid money as there was practically none to be had for this purpose. If there was any silver or gold coin, it was used to purchase hardware needed for the structure being erected.

This industrious zeal prevailed throughout the community. Little time was spent on frivolity. Clean living and hard work were usually rewarded with long life. Many of the people of yesterday lived to ripe old ages. They carried on their lives with the strictest moral standards and most of the social values we respect in modern times. As most of the perishable food was heavily salted, this may or may not have been a factor in their health. One reason offered for the longevity of Cape Codders was that "they were well preserved in their salt." But a quick look through the old Cape cemetaries revealed that some people died in their 30's and 40's. It cannot be determined if excessive salt in their diets had an effect on the length of their lives. Some men had the reputation for being "salty" but that was usually in reference to the language used by sailors.

*History of Levi Crowell, copyright 1990 by Wm. Smith Ryder, Jr.

This photograph is from the collection of David Sears of Quivet Neck in East Dennis. Although there is no specific identification with the picture it is believed to be the saltworks of John Sears. In the center of the photograph there are two people sitting on the fence and two others are standing to the left. It is probably a sunny day as all of the vats are open.

The Development
of Solar Evaporation

Recognition for the first successful solar-evaporation saltworks on Cape Cod is credited to Captain John Sears of Dennis. Captain Sears was a fifth generation descendant of Richard Sears, one of the early Yarmouth settlers. The Captain earned the nickname of "Sleepy John Sears" because, like many literate men, he would sit and think for long periods of time. People thought him asleep when they called and he did not answer. They began to call him "Sleepy John" and after the success of his invention they called him "Salt John."

A study of the Sears genealogy reveals that the saltworks inventor descended from Richard Sears through his son Paul. From the second generation Paul, came John in the third generation; another named John, the fourth generation and then Captain John Sears was the fifth generation. He was born in Yarmouth on July 20, 1744 and died in Dennis on June 9, 1817. He married Phebe Sears, the daughter of a distant relative, on December 26, 1771, in Yarmouth. Phebe was born on March 31, 1747 and died in January, 1818. They had nine children, all of whom lived to adulthood, although their third child, Daniel, born in 1777, died at sea when he was twenty years old. The other children were Olive (1772), Deborah (1774), Heman (1780), Jerusha (1781), Enos (1783), Lavinia (1785), Moody (1788), and Fanny (1791). The last direct descendant of John Sears died a few years ago in East Dennis.

Captain Sears began his experiments with solar evaporation to

This picture shows the remains of the British Man-Of-War *Somerset* on Peaked Hill Bars in Provincetown. The ship was wrecked in 1778 and the hull was burned. The only evidence left was a few charred bones but the durability of English oak is represented by these pieces, in a photograph of the remains, taken over two hundred years after the wreck. *Photo by William P. Quinn.*

obtain salt, in 1776, at Quivet Neck, on Sesuit Harbor, in what is now East Dennis. He built a "large trough ten feet wide and a hundred feet long with a series of shutters to cover the vats when it rained." One flaw in the operation was that the trough leaked and after many weeks of work the yield was only eight bushels of salt. The good citizens of Quivet Neck were skeptical. They called his experiment "Sears Folly." Captain Sears, however, was not disheartened. During the winter, being a good sailor, he caulked his vats to stop the leaks. The following summer, he obtained thirty bushels of salt and this progress did not escape the attention of his neighbors. Unfortunately, the labor involved in the manufacture was toilsome. All of the water for the vats had to be carried by hand in pails from the nearby shore. But, undaunted, Captain Sears continued his work.

In a northeast storm on November 2, 1778, during the Revolutionary War, the British Man-Of-War *Somerset,* was wrecked on

Peaked Hill Bars at Provincetown. The salvagers in the lower Cape towns stripped everything of value from the hull following the wreck. There were no aids to navigation around Cape Cod at this time and wrecks were commonplace. Wrecking and salvage were profitable trades here. Captain Sears obtained one of the bilge pumps from the warship and used it to supply water for his saltworks. The pump alleviated the manual labor of carrying the water in buckets. This improvement helped, but there was still a large amount of physical exertion involved in working the pump. The cost of producing the salt far exceeded the return and the labor must have been exhausting. But Captain Sears persevered.

The development of the salt works on Cape Cod occurred over a period of twenty years between 1776 and 1796. A few years after the initial efforts began, Major Nathaniel Freeman of Harwich suggested using wind power to pump water up into the vats. Captain Sears set small pumps atop wood framed structures. The wind vanes carried about six yards of canvas on each blade. These picturesque machines were called salt mills. They pumped salt water through hollowed out pine logs, made water-tight with white lead. At all saltworks, part of the piping system was buried below tide level in the Cape sands and over the years, the salt water preserved the wood very well. In recent times, a few of these wooden pipes have been dug up along the shore and found to be in surprisingly good condition. The windmill idea was a significant breakthrough in the technology. This new concept eliminated all of the back-breaking labor in transporting the salt water and the business began to show a profit. A few years later, Mr. Hattil Kelley of Dennis built a new kind of vat with sliding covers and called it a crane works. His idea was to erect the works in a checkerboard fashion. He set up a series of two vats with two covers supported by a single framework. This further reduced the labor involved and another improvement was recorded. Mr. Kelley later got a patent for his idea.

Another cover was invented in 1793 by Reuben Sears, a carpenter from Harwich. His contribution to the industry was a simple sliding square roof which ran back and forth on rollers. The rollers were made out of oak and were durable enough to stand up under continued use. Security lashings

This group of vats was part of a vast spread in South Yarmouth and depicts both types of saltworks; crane works and vats with sliding roofs. Along the right side of the photograph are the hollowed out logs used to pump water to the vats. The vat in the foreground on the right side of the picture had a sliding roof but the two vats directly behind it were crane works. The beam connecting the two roofs is the support between them while the man on the left side appears to be moving the roofs of another set of crane works. *Photo courtesy of Alec & Audrey Todd, Yarmouth, Mass.*

were used to tie the roofs down in case of high winds or adverse weather. The sliding roof cover was commonly adapted to most of the Cape Cod saltworks. The Reverend Ephraim Briggs of Chatham was a proficient chemist and he assisted with technology in the manufacturing process. There were other men with various ideas and improvements but the basic plan employed was in keeping with the original concept of the process. Full development of the saltworks was finally realized over several years and just before 1800, the industry began to grow at a rapid rate.

The evaporation of sea water to make salt was carried on only during the months of March through October. The vats were covered each night and during days whenever rain clouds threatened. Where large areas of vats had to be covered, it was often a group effort. Several persons (even the housewives), rolled the roofs over the open vats. When a large number of people were covering the vats together, the sound was quite often similar to that of distant thunder. If a summer shower threatened, the entire town, men, women and children, joined together to preserve the evaporation already completed.

There is no one alive today who can remember seeing any of the Cape Cod saltworks. The last trace of any remains was torn down over one hundred years ago. There are, at this period of time, some who can remember stories, told in early childhood, by their parents. Josephine Robinson Lakin of South Yarmouth was born in 1912 and recalls her mother, Lottie Chapman, telling about operations at the local saltworks. When it started to rain she (Lottie), her brother, and her sister would rush to cover the vats. All the children in the neighborhood would take part in this activity. She added that it took at least two youngsters to roll one roof. In the spring and fall, children were sent from school to help protect the salt. The saltworks, while privately owned, were considered the bread and butter of the community and everyone helped when they could. In 1783, after the Revolutionary War had shut off the supply of imported salt for the fishing industry, the local price quickly escalated from fifty cents to eight dollars a bushel.

Captain Sears improved his works during the years after the war and, as the price per bushel came down, better technology improved the yield. It normally required 350 gallons of sea water to make one bushel of Cape Cod sea salt. A bushel weighed about eighty pounds but this varied with the purity of the product. The process of evaporation usually took about three weeks to complete, depending on the weather. Because of the improved technology, this salt was superior to the product obtained by boiling sea water. Captain Sears was assisted in his development by Captains William Crowell, Christopher Crowell, and Edward Sears. These men, all sea captains living in East Dennis, worked together. It is, therefore, reasonable to surmise that much of the practical knowledge for the process had been brought home from abroad. Salt was manufactured in the

Above: The Dennis Bicentennial Commission dedicated a monument to John Sears in 1976. The boulder lies in the center of a field where some of the Sears saltworks were situated. **Below:** The bronze plaque is about Mr. Sears who is considered the progenitor of this early industry. *Photo by William P. Quinn.*

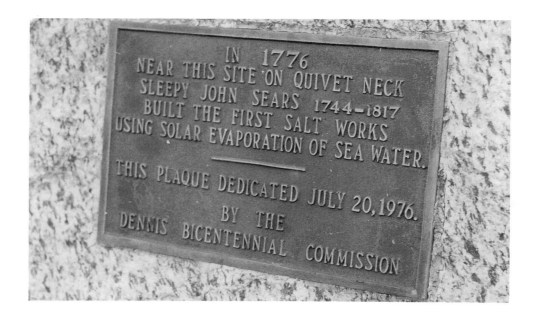

Saltworks were situated near coastal estuaries where salt mills pumped the sea water up to the vats for evaporation. In this photograph, two pair of tandem mills worked together to raise the salt water for a saltworks located back from the shore on a higher level. *Photo courtesy of the Brewster Historical Society.*

Caribbean and in southern Europe by the evaporation method using salt pans (salt pans are hollows cut in the ground and lined with clay so they won't leak).

The knowledge of saltworks from abroad, however, did not prevent Captain John Sears from obtaining a patent for his invention in 1799. The other three captains had signed over their rights and title to the invention. The patent was disputed by others who claimed that "no new development" had been made. There was no doubt that the evaporation process itself was not new but the salt vats manufactured in Dennis by Captain Sears were different. And remember, from 1776 through those long years of development, Captain John Sears had persevered. Credit for the creation of the industry on Cape Cod was his alone. More importantly, the new invention also met the local needs for a scarce commodity. Doubts as to the validity of the patent, however, continued. Amos Otis, Jr., wrote in April,

1832: "Mr. Sears obtained a patent for his salt works, and Mr. Kelly for his improvement; they united their claims, but, after much litigation in the Federal Court, lost their case, and the exclusive benefit of their inventions."

The practical application of this technology began its phenomenal growth after 1797. John Sears was able to utilize his knowledge and became successful with his idea at that time. The contest against the patent in the Federal courts was later successful because of a lack of proper defense by Sears' attorneys. The partnership of John and Edward Sears, Christopher and William Crowell carried on the business and the patent challenge charged that one of the partners, William Crowell, had examined a salt works erected on the Isle of Shoals off the coast of New Hampshire and that the Sears works embraced the same principle. It was apparent that lawyers did not prosecute any further testimony about the Isle of Shoals operations because it was later proved that no salt had ever been made there, by solar evaporation, prior to 1800.

Many changes on the peninsula were brought about by the rapid development of the saltworks. The barren seaside on Cape Cod was considered wild land by the original settlers. Its primary use was in the salt marshes for cutting hay to feed cattle. The use of these areas was extensive by the farmers. None of the saltworks was built on any area of salt marsh. One reason for this restriction was the belief that the process of evaporation would have been impeded by the damp ground.

The Cape's upland beach areas had been left mostly in their natural state until the saltworks construction began. This widespread building completely changed the seaside landscape. The prolific use of these natural areas created a new rural scenery with covered vats as far as the eye could see. Construction of this type and magnitude would be completely inconsistent with today's building codes, zoning regulations and environmental laws. But in that era, the desire for profit and some inherent common sense overruled esthetic considerations. The vats, that were constructed during the early years, cost about a hundred to one hundred twenty-five dollars for one hundred square feet. From this, cost of the wood and other materials amounted to about two thirds, and the balance was for labor. The business began to multiply rapidly after several improvements had been implemented. Just before 1800, saltworks were being constructed all over Cape Cod. The return on the investment was estimated to be between 25 and 30 percent which was remarkable for those times.

Most all of Captain Sears' neighbors became involved in building saltworks. Simeon Deyo's <u>History</u> <u>of</u> <u>Barnstable</u> <u>County</u> (1890) told about the early activities at the Cape saltworks: "The entire surface of Quivet neck adjoining the bay, and the greater part of Sesuet, were covered with vats. Of the Sears and Crowell families, the first on the neck, nearly all the heads engaged in this work." This is somewhat of an exaggeration as the Quivet Neck map clearly shows. The "entire surface" was not covered. But, a large area was utilized for the manufacture of salt.

Cape Cod was the perfect location for this industry. Indeed, the water was saltier because of the extension of the peninsula out into the Atlantic. It was a good distance from the coastline where rivers emptying into the ocean dilute the sea water. The upland area along the Cape Cod shorelines was conducive to this type of activity. Long dry summer days with a hot sun, high in the sky, contributed greatly to the evaporation. On damp muggy days the process of evaporation was retarded a great deal but not completely. The evaporation process had no effect on the local weather. Cape Cod is surrounded by hundreds of square miles of ocean and natural evaporation goes on constantly around this narrow peninsula while Mother Nature's colossal distillery works its wonders. The composition of sea water contains about 3.5 percent solids by weight. Of these, sodium chloride has the largest percentage, 2.68 percent. Others by weight: magnesium chloride, .32 percent; magnesium sulfate, .22 percent; calcium sulfate, .12 percent; potassium chloride, .07 percent and sodium bromide, .008 percent. The remaining .82 percent, is comprised of some forty plus elements dissolved in sea water. There is even a trace of gold among these. With the above breakdown of percentages it was not an easy task to produce pure salt. All of the impurities had to be removed and most of these were but there was a tiny amount of lime in most of the salt produced on Cape Cod. This, however, was minute and did not affect the quality. After 1829, new

An 1849 map of Quivet Neck shows the large concentration of saltworks spread out on the land. The areas marked with a checkerboard depict the locations of the saltworks. The illustration reveals that the entire surface of the neck was not covered with vats but a large acreage was used for evaporaters. To locate the landmarks, the road running east and west along the bottom of the map is the present highway designated Route 6A in East Dennis.

An aerial photograph looking north in the Quivet Neck area at Dennis as it looks today, showing the lands where many of the saltworks were located. The road running east and west in the center of the picture is called Saltworks Road. *Aerial Photo by William P. Quinn.*

Massachusetts laws required that salt be checked by state inspectors for purity.

The procedure was relatively simple and effective. The saltworks vats were ten to sixteen feet square and between nine and twelve inches deep. The process involved sometimes three different levels to obtain the needed salt. The first vat was the water room where sea animals and some plant life were precipitated. The second was the pickle room where much of the lime came out. The third vat was the salt room. The three vats were situated one below the other. Gravity achieved the transfer of the brine in the three steps required to complete the process. The long low areas surrounding the dry sandy shores were natural sites for the industry. Nothing was wasted. The precipitate from the first vat was sometimes used as fertilizer on the farms. Further treatment of the "bitter water" after the salt was extracted produced Glauber and Epsom salts.

After the initial investment, maintenance costs were minimal. These were principally to pay for repairs from any storm damage that might occur. Other expenses were for one or two men to run the works in the summer. These were usually older men or young boys because the working adults were either tending to farm chores or out fishing to help support the family. By the year 1800, the expansion of the salt business had started many on the road to prosperity around Cape Cod. The process was one of small investment, where Mother Nature supplied most of the labor and the raw materials were free. The salt works were dubbed "the lazy man's gold mine." Day to day operations at the saltworks were not overly exciting. Wind powered pumps raised the sea water, the sun supplied the heat for evaporation and gravity was used to pass the brine down from one vat to the next. The operator had only to shovel the damp salt out of the vats and bring it to a drying room. The sodium chloride precipitated out in large crystals. While suitable in this form for the salting of fish, it was necessary to grind the large crystals for use in the home.

The salt vats were measured by the foot. A vat ten feet square was considered to be 10 running feet of works. The tax assessor listed the measurements in "superficial feet" and this term was used for the amount of footage in any given saltworks. The measurement of one superficial foot was described as one foot wide by ten feet deep, thus if a man had ten vats, each ten feet square, he had one hundred superficial feet of works. In 1802, there were 136 saltworks in the county of Barnstable containing 121,313 superficial feet. The product of these plants was estimated to have a value of $41,000. After thirty years, the business had increased to 881 saltworks containing 1,414,608 superficial feet producing over 250,000 bushels of salt annually. Some of the 1851 maps show the proliferation of salt-vats along the Cape's coastal zone. Near the peak of operations, there were over two million dollars invested in the salt industry on Cape Cod. Clearly, this manufacture was one of the major factors in the Cape's economy. About this same time, there was a related business carried on in Eastham. A magnesia factory was operated during the salt era. Magnesia is a by-product of the salt industry. Eastham Town records indicated that it was assessed for $200 and later the assessment went up to $325. There was another magnesia plant in South Yarmouth doing business in the 1850's.

The rapid development of salt-making was closely correlated to the growth of the fishing fleet because salt was used to preserve the fish caught off shore. Thoreau called Cape Cod the "bared and bended arm of Massachusetts." That "arm" extended well into the Atlantic. The locale of the peninsula, forty miles out, stationed the fishermen of Cape Cod conveniently nearer to the fishing grounds. The fishing industry had modest beginnings here but grew rapidly with the Caribbean trade. The Cape fishermen filled their holds on the Grand Banks. They sailed home as fast as the winds allowed and dried their fish on flakes erected near the beach. After the fish was salted and stowed, the ships set sail for the West Indies to trade for sugar, salt, cotton, molasses and rum. Others who did not trade south could find a ready market for their salt cured fish in Boston. The Revolutionary War at first severely restricted this trade and later halted it completely.

During the Revolutionary War, the British seized many American vessels at sea and impressed their crews into the Royal Navy. For seven years, most of the fishing boats lay in Cape Cod harbors, rotting. A period of economic depression set in following the war and lasted well into 1789. When the Constitution was ratified, tariff laws were clarified, protecting the saltmakers from imported salt. After the war, there was very little left for the Cape Cod fisherman. But the Yankee acumen prevailed. New fishing boats were built; the men returned to the fishing grounds and business began to improve again albeit with measured steps. The foreign supplies of salt were cut off but the Cape Cod saltworks industry had, by this time, developed enough to meet the demand of the local fishing industry. The transition took place slowly to met the challenge.

The government was not slow in recognizing that a need must be filled. The Massachusetts General Court decreed that "to encourage the manufacture of salt, a bounty of three shillings per bushel be paid by the state treasury for salt manufactured within the state and produced from sea water." It was very soon after this that the industry began to assume

An artists conception of a typical Cape Cod saltworks in the early nineteenth century. The evaporators were constructed near the shores of coves and inlets. This ideal location afforded proximity to wharfs where fishing vessels and coastal traders could tie up and load salt casks. *Drawing by Paul C. Morris, Nantucket, Mass.*

significant proportions economically. With the wily Cape Codders, a keen eye is always on the lookout for a dollar and, where there is one to be made, many more can be found for investment. In the year 1802, saltworks had begun to cover the shorelines in the bayside towns of Brewster, Dennis, Yarmouth and Barnstable. Almost anyone with a couple of acres near a tidal stream erected his own works. The resulting growth of this industry in the thirty years following 1800 was phenomenal. Land was not a problem for descendants of the early settlers as the common fields were part of the Proprietary rights granted, in perpetuity, to the first families and all their heirs on Cape Cod during the 1640's. This included all the wild and undeveloped lands, beaches and flats. A large portion of the waterfront upland around Cape Cod was part of this description. This land had been

This photograph is from the collections at the Library of Congress in Washington, D.C., and shows saltworks in Chatham. The picture was probably made in the 1860's because it appears that the vats were not being maintained.

purchased from the native Americans on Cape Cod by the ancient Proprietors. In the early 1700's, the land was divided among the original settlers and remained for several years as common lands in the colony.*

During his travels through the northern United States, a Mr. Edward Augustus Kimball in 1808 wrote an interesting narrative of life on Cape Cod for that period. Mr. Kimball arrived in Barnstable one evening and spent the night. His narrative described the visit: "The next morning, I breakfasted at a public house near the court-house, which is small, but surrounded by several lawyers' offices. Only the female part of the family were in the house, the men of all the neighbourhood being at work in the marshes, making salt hay. The former told me that they were at a second breakfast, having taken a first at three o'clock in the morning, when they made tea for the men, before their going to work."

*See Page 31

Mr. Kimball then traveled to Chatham where he met Mr. Richard Sears, the owner of extensive saltworks. He described the process:

"The manufacture of the process of which the following is the outline, is sea salt, obtained from sea water, by evaporation, artificially forwarded. The water, being raised by a pump that is placed a little below high-water mark, is led by troughs into a range of vats or rooms, distinguished by the name of 'water-rooms.' In these, it remains for a longer or shorter period, accordingly as the atmosphere happens to be more or less favourable to evaporation, till at length it arrives at the state that satisfies the judgment of the manufacturer: under the best circumstances, the usual period is three days; but, under others, it is six. From the water-rooms, it is drawn into a second range of vats or rooms, called pickle-rooms, the strength of the water being now such as to constitute it a brine or pickle. Here, it deposits a large proportion of lime and other earthy matter; and here small cubical crystals of salt, resembling fine grains of sand, begin to form upon the surface. This appearance is the signal for a third remove; and the water is now drawn into the last range of vats or rooms, called salt-rooms. Here the crystals, conglomerating, continue to form, and compose large and heavy cubes, which sink to the bottom or floor of the vat. The salt, which is now complete, having accumulated on the floors, is raked together, taken out of the vats, and deposited in a dry warehouse. The entire period of the process is usually about three weeks."

There are several descriptions of the process and most are similar in context but one of the better scientific accounts is that one given by James Thacher in 1802. His paper appears in the appendix.

Unfortunately, none of the old saltworks was saved or preserved for posterity. There are two small salt vats at the Aptuxet Trading Post at Bourne which were built in modern times as an historic display for the tourists. These are not used to evaporate salt water but to depict the ancient art of salt manufacture. At Chatham, the Historical Society has a small model of an old saltworks in their museum. If man could harness and use solar energy today with the same degree of efficiency as the old time salt makers did, civilization could abandon its dependency on fossil fuels and enrich the environment where we live but man will probably continue this use until those fuels are exhausted.

In 1927, Attorney Samuel D. Hannah of Buzzards Bay tried to reestablish the rights from the Proprietary Corporations of the Ancient Cape Cod towns and create titles to undeveloped lands. The lands were deeded to the Proprietors and their descendants in the early days of the settlements in Barnstable County. The deeds were supposed to be in perpetuity so that theoretically, Mr. Hannah contended, anyone who could prove that he or she descended from the first comers was entitled to all rights enjoyed by their forefathers. The Barnstable County court house burned in 1827 and many vital records were lost at that time. Title searches for all these many lands would propose a formidable task for any lawyer today but a case was presented to the Supreme Court in 1928 which may have settled any claims present day heirs may have. The Judge ruled that any resurrection of Proprietor's claims were invalid. He said: "the Proprietors were corporations which were supposed to die when they had conveyed all their lands." A successful challenge to this decision today would create a multitude of legal problems in Barnstable County.

*From: Cape Cod History & Genealogy, C.W. Swift, publisher & printer, 1927

"Permissive uses of the common lands of proprietary plantations.

"The modern theory was that: There was no adverse use of Common Lands because all Proprietors in a township were allowed to use the land for their own private purposes so long as there were no permanent structures erected and maintained beyond a period when the land and building could be used with profit. This permission often extended to the use of the inhabitants although they were not Proprietors

"The uses made of common areas, particularly beach, meaning what in modern terms is called beach upland, were numerous. The most common use was the drying and stacking of salt hay, sedge and thatch; then there were stages for the curing of fish in the air and sun - or the drying places called "flake fields," where the fish after splitting and salting were spread out over a large area on sticks or boards. Then there were landing places - sometimes docks built of piling and boarding. Later the salt industry developed and salt works were erected, usually on the back side of a beach near salt water ponds, from which the salt water was pumped into evaporating vats.

"Try houses where fish and blubber were boiled in order to procure the oil was a common process in the early days, and extended to a time not beyond the memory of some persons now living. Sometimes this process was carried on under the shelter of a roofed structure or it might be done in the open.

"Still another use was the burning of lime from shells which were in large heaps, left by the Indians over a period of centuries.

"The making of tar at one time was not an uncommon industry. The Proprietors of the common wood land frequently gave permission within restricted areas to box the pines, collect the sap and treat it on the premises to separate the resin and the tar, or it might be done by a heating process applied to pine knots. For this privilege a rental was sometimes paid to the Proprietee and distributed to the Proprietors.

"Because of these permissive uses of common lands allowed to the public in general no taxes were ever paid by the Proprietary corporations within Plymouth Colony even after the creation of the Province and the Commonwealth. The towns populations grew and later outnumbered the original Proprietors and the rights and privleges of same were soon left behind."

Expansion of the

Salt Trade

Chapter Three

At the beginning of the 19th century, the manufacture of salt was one of the primary movers of a flourishing maritime trade sailing out of Cape Cod ports. What followed was a gradual transition from a fishing and agricultural economy to a fishing, trading and industrial one. This development extended over a long period of time. The farming and fishing on the Cape underwent a transformation to one of more dependency upon the fishing industry as the soil exhaustion of the land sent more men to sea. The saltworks were vital to the fishing fleet and this spawned other industries which were interdependent upon one another and more trade resulted to enrich the businessmen of Cape Cod.

When the Pilgrims first arrived in this country, survival was arduous and rooted in an agricultural way of life. The Pilgrims had to learn how to grow corn and fertilize their crops. With the help of friendly Indians, they learned to produce the food they needed. Their settlement in Plymouth was on land formerly of an Indian tribe that had been exterminated by a smallpox epidemic a few years before the Pilgrims arrived.

By the eighteenth century, with hard work, farmers provided ample food for their families and the surplus was exported to off-Cape markets. In addition to the crops, livestock became another important adjunct to the farm and provided part of the farmer's income. The man and woman of the house were usually engaged in continuous labor to keep the family going. There was little time for idleness. When one job was done, another was

A typical Cape Cod fishing vessel under full sail headed for the banks. The trip usually lasted anywhere from two to four weeks in order to load the hold with codfish. It was a hard way to make a living but hundreds of men went to sea and fished the Grand Banks.

begun. The ingrained work ethic was passed along from parent to child.

After the fall harvest, men engaged in other types of work. Some went fishing while many others were skilled craftsmen. They built ships, boats or houses during the long winter months. In the early 1800's, there were increasing problems with the topsoil on Cape Cod. The prime forests that existed here in the seventeenth century were cut down to make larger farms and to provide lumber for homes and shipbuilding. Bigger farms and overproduction resulted in less fertile soil. The crop yield declined noticeably from this depletion. Loose topsoil was further eroded by the wind, causing silting of many harbors. This had a negative effect on shellfishing. During the Revolutionary War, many of the fishermen had to stay ashore. They started farming in order to make a living and this created further enervation of the land. Toward the end of the eighteenth century, these environmental changes created problems for many farmers. Some of the men who lived near the shores and salt water estuaries built saltworks while others further inland had to find better ways to fertilize their land in order to grow their food. Undaunted, the Yankee spirit of freedom prevailed and they searched for better solutions to their problems. Some farmers utilized the Cape's plentiful supply of shellfish to fertilize their crops.

Another quote from Edward A. Kimball's travels on Cape Cod in 1808 described his view of lower Cape scenes. On his way from Truro to Provincetown he wrote about the farmers and their fertilizer: "For a short space, the road lay over hills, on which were crops of maize, now nearly ready for harvest. The favourite manure is the king or horseshoe crab, of which there are great numbers on the coast; and to each hill, that is to each three plants, there is allotted one crab, divested of its shell. The sand, thus nourished, yields an adequate return for the labours of the husbandman; the grain filling well, though the plant is of very low stature, and in a great degree without its broad and ornamental flag-like leaves."

Cape Cod's industrial growth was anchored to the fishing industry and fluctuations in that business, up or down, were reflected in other trades. During the proliferation of the salt industry, the related businesses

A photograph taken in the late nineteenth century at Provincetown with three coastal traders tied up next to the pier. One of these vessels could carry more cargo than could be loaded on a large modern eighteen-wheel tractor-trailer truck of today. *Photo courtesy of Cape Cod Photos, Orleans, Mass.*

prospered too, especially the packet boats. Not to be confused with the Atlantic Packet ships, these were the small freight and passenger carriers between the Cape and Boston. The packet vessels provided a local connection for overseas commerce but this was a very minor part of the business. A good portion of the salt manufactured on Cape Cod was consumed locally by the fishing fleet but the surplus was shipped to Boston or New York on the coasters and packets, but, not everyone made salt. There were several other related occupations in the maritime field here. Ship building was carried on in most all of the towns on the Cape and this activity propagated many different trades for the local people. Some of these included the manufacture of ship's masts, hardware, rope, sails, barrels, nets and small boats. It was all inclusive for the maritime trades.

Because of the hundreds of fishing, packet and coastal freight vessels owned on Cape Cod, the waterfront villages were busy centers of activity almost every day throughout the year, particularly during the fall harvest time. Business was thriving and prosperity was widespread throughout Barnstable county. The products of ocean and farm comprised the bulk of cargoes carried by the coasters from the Maritimes to the Caribbean. But glass, clothing, bricks, fertilizer and salt were also manufactured on the Cape for export. In 1802, Falmouth had fifty-four sailing vessels engaged in the coastal trade from the Canadian maritimes south to the Carolinas. These boats averaged about 55 gross tons. (This compares in size with a modern day fishing dragger of about fifty to sixty feet in length.) It was during this period that major physical changes were made in many coastal towns with the building of wharves and docks to accommodate the loading of the packets and coastal schooners. The construction of these large piers provided a home to several associated trades. Sail lofts, blacksmith and ship's-carpenter shops were situated right on the dock to facilitate maintenance and repairs while the vessels were alongside. The proximity to the new piers expedited the loading of salt and other cargoes into the ships.

This activity brought other business to the neighborhoods: tin smiths, ship-chandlers and spar yards established their workshops close to the waterfront. In 1814, the Nobscusset Point Pier was built in Dennis. A stone and timber structure, it extended six hundred feet out into Cape Cod Bay. Wooden pile wharfs began in the 1820's. Whaling was at its peak in the first half of the nineteenth century and, in addition, a large mackerel fishing fleet sailed out of Wellfleet. The maintainence and provisioning of these vessels added to the already busy waterfront areas. There were several deepwater ships owned in the outer Cape towns. These vessels made voyages to the West Indies, South America, Australia, India and eastern Asia. It was once written that there were more sea captain's houses along the main road in Brewster than any other town in the land. Many of these mansions still stand along the present Route 6A in that town.

Every town on the bay shores had its own packet. A few had two or sometimes three boats on the Boston route. The towns on the south shore of the Cape had coastal vessels sailing to New Bedford, continuing into Long Island Sound, and thence to ports in Connecticut and New York City. These coasters were chiefly freight vessels. It is possible that an occasional passenger was carried but this was rare. With the passage of time, navigational aids were developed around the Cape in the form of lighthouses and buoys. The sailor was also assisted by more accurate charts. Storms and fog, however, continued to take a heavy toll in shipwrecks.

The packets were the lifeline of the Cape for both passengers and commerce. They were preferred universally over the early stagecoaches, those back straining, rough riding, overland transports that rambled over bad roads and forded streams through the south shore towns between Boston and Cape Cod. Stagecoach travel was never too popular with the Cape people and was undertaken only in times of emergency, in winter, or when the packets were held in port because of repairs or bad weather. "Going to Boston by land was less common than a voyage to China."* However, in any group of people, there are those who have different opinions. These preferred the stage over water travel because they were afraid of being shipwrecked.

*Shebna Rich <u>Landmarks</u> <u>and</u> <u>Sea Marks, Truro, Cape Cod, 1884.</u>

There was one pleasant interlude during the stagecoach journey. The several taverns along the route were temporary layovers in order to change horses and to give the passengers a chance to stretch their legs. There were other niceties about these stops as described in Deyo's History: "A good meal and a hot toddy, in the days before the temperance movement had been inaugurated, left pleasant recollections of the place left behind, and excited agreeable anticipations of the next one to come." One of the taverns on Cape Cod was located in Barnstable on what is the present Route 6A. This was the Crocker Tavern. An ordinary and the gathering place of local citizens. Evenings, over a tankard of beer, friendly arguments sometimes occured over politics, taxes, and the price of corn or salt. Cornelius Crocker was the host and the stagecoaches stopped here regularly. The old roadhouse still stands and is presently a Bed & Breakfast residence, catering to the summer tourists, continuing with a similar business that began there in the late eighteenth century. The only other method of transportation to the city was by horseback but the time required for the ride and the discomfort endured ruled out all except the most hardy men.

The steam packet *Chancellor Livingston* was one of the vessels on the Providence to New York run in the 1830's. This steamer and three others maintained a schedule for passengers and freight between the two ports.

For those wanting passage to New York City, there was a steam packet line running through Long Island Sound. The first part of the trip was by stagecoach from Boston. Cape Codders either had to take a stage to Boston or sail on the packet; spend the night and get up early the next morning. The stage left Boston at five a.m. (except Sunday) and the steamer left Providence, Rhode Island at noon for New York. An advertisement appeared in the Daily Evening Transcript at Boston on September 30, 1830 for the New York and Boston Steam Packet Line. The fare was five dollars and a steamboat carried the passengers from Providence, to New York City.

There were four steamboats on the line to New York: the *Benjamin Franklin*, the *Chancellor Livingston*, the *Washington*, and the *President*. Dinner was served on board the steamers for 50 cents; breakfast and tea was 38 cents. The era of steamboat travel had just begun and the early steam engines were not always reliable. There was the risk of a boiler explosion on board at any time.

When Henry David Thoreau travelled from Sandwich to Orleans in 1849, he felt the stagecoach was too narrow for the nine people crammed inside. The journey along the peninsula was published in his lengthy essay entitled Cape Cod. He wrote:

"This coach was an exceedingly narrow one, but as there was a slight spherical excess over two on a seat, the driver waited till nine passengers had got in, without taking the measure of any of them, and then shut the door after two or three ineffectual slams, as if the fault were all in the hinges or the latch, - while we timed our inspirations and expirations so as to assist him."

Thoreau described classically, and at some length, the towns as they drove through them but did not dwell on the discomfort endured by those in the coach. His long trip began on a train from Boston to Sandwich and then in a stagecoach to Orleans. Thoreau was disappointed that the coach did not stop at any tavern along the way. Perhaps a tankard of "Flip" might have softened his disposition and possibly changed his observations about the countryside. He wrote about the ride through Dennis and mentioned seeing the roofs of Captain John Sears' saltworks (Captain Sears, however, had passed away in 1817). From Orleans, he walked the rest of the way to Provincetown in order to get closer to nature. The narration in the book detailed his trek over the dunes and beaches to the tip of the Cape. He had a perceptive notion for the lands he had traversed.

"The time must come when this coast will be a place of resort for those New-Englanders who really wish to visit the seaside. At present it is wholly unknown to the fashionable world, and probably it will never be agreeable to them. If it is merely a ten-pin alley, or a circular railway, or an ocean of mint-julep, that the visitor is in search of, - if he thinks more of the wine than the brine, as I suspect some do at Newport, - I trust that for a long time he will be disappointed here.

"But this shore will never be more attractive than it is now. Such beaches as are fashionable are here made and unmade in a day, I may almost say, by the sea shifting its sands. Lynn and Nantasket! this bare and bended arm it is that makes the bay in which they lie so snugly. What are springs and waterfalls? Here is the spring of springs, the waterfall of waterfalls. A storm in the fall or winter is the time to visit it; a light-house or a fisherman's hut the true hotel. A man may stand there and put all America behind him."

Thoreau's concept in 1857 has come true, even to a greater degree than he could ever have envisioned. He would not, however, look favorably on Cape Cod the way it has been developed today. The peninsula has grown in the 20th century to where tourists have replaced the saltworks, fishing, and most all of the other industries. Thoreau's "Cape Cod" is still there, however, if one knows where to look for it. The beauty and solitude of the outer shore has changed little. It may not be a "spring of springs" any more but a walk on the beach is still an opiate for lovers of nature. The coast is continually eroded by storm and surf and there is little man can do to change this. The ocean has profiled the shoreline here since it was formed by the glaciers. This will probably continue into eternity, as will the popularity of Thoreau's book.

At the beginning of the nineteenth century, there were events that contributed to changes in the history of Cape Cod. The technology for the manufacture of salt had progressed to the point where this industry had become one of the dominant factors in the local economy. Tragedy struck during the winter of 1800-1801 when a smallpox epidemic raged all over the Cape; many persons lost their lives. In spite of the epidemic, the population of Barnstable County increased by five thousand persons during the twenty years between 1790 and 1810. This was probably due to the prodigious

The elegant mansion of Captain Ebenezer Harding Linnell on Skaket Road in Orleans. In the present time (1992) it is the Captain Linnell House Restaurant. *Photo by H.K. Cummings.*

economic growth in the county. The scourge also wiped out most of the remaining Indian population here. The Indians, however, left their mark on Cape Cod. As was the practice throughout New England, every town on this peninsula has a few names left over from the early tribes. Most of these are difficult to pronounce while several are almost impossible to spell.

Nearly every port in the world was familiar to seafarers from Cape Cod. After the deep sea captains made their fortunes, they came home from their ocean travels and swallowed the anchor (retired). Many of these men invested their money in saltworks. Their small Cape cottages were later enlarged into luxurious mansions, copied from ones seen on their travels around the world. Some of these still stand to this day. One beautiful example of this is the Captain Linnell House on Skaket Road in Orleans, which today is an elegant restaurant. At the beginning of the nineteenth century, every business prospered but there was an obstacle looming that would put a temporary cramp in this growth.

An artists conception of a busy day at the harbor. The drawing depicts a hogshead of salt being loaded aboard a coastal schooner using a horse for power to lift the heavy load. This scene could have been at any one of a dozen ports around Cape Cod. *Drawing by Paul C. Morris, Nantucket, Mass.*

The War of 1812 dealt a near fatal blow to the expanding industrial progress on Cape Cod. It began in 1807 when the 40-gun United States Frigate *Chesapeake* was hailed by the 50-gun British Frigate *Leopard* off Virginia coast. A surprise attack by the British killed three crewmen and wounded eighteen. Four men were impressed off the American ship. The badly damaged *Chesapeake* limped back into Norfolk. The news of the attack infuriated the nation and the people demanded revenge. President Thomas Jefferson did not have an army or navy ready for war. His only weapon was an embargo of American goods being traded with any foreign country. The result was catastrophic for the local economy and had little effect on either France or Britain, the two countries Jefferson was trying to punish.

The people engaged in trade once again resorted to smuggling as was done with a large degree of success prior to the Revolution. The illegal transfer of goods was rife and several persons were brought before the courts only to be released by sympathetic judges and juries. One Cape Cod coasting Captain loaded his vessel with several barrels of water and told the inspectors how people in Boston had asked for Cape Cod water whenever he came into that port. The authorities were not fooled. It was obvious that the water was to be traded to a British vessel just out of sight off shore.

The embargo, however, proved to be a welcome stimulant to the salt industry on Cape Cod. With the foreign ports closed, the price of salt here was inflated to seven dollars a bushel. When shipbuilding was curtailed, this capital was invested on the local level, mostly to erect more saltworks. From 1802 to 1810 the capacity of salt manufacturing doubled on the Cape. Barnstable County had about 70 percent of all the works in Massachusetts and Bristol County had nearly 24 percent. There were additional saltworks on the island of Martha's Vineyard. An attempt was made at Nantucket but later abandoned because of the ubiquitous fogs which kept the air moist and prevented the suns rays from evaporating the sea water with any degree of success. Between 1810 and 1831 the capacity of the Cape's saltworks rose over 300 percent. The erection and repair work of the vats employed a substantial number of Cape Codders. The War of 1812 reduced the maritime travel between Cape Cod and Boston to a trickle. Overland travel by horse and wagon was one way to escape the English blockade along the coast. The land freight business was slower and more expensive but during the conflict, it was the only safe way to get a cargo into the city without risk of the capture and ultimate loss of the goods.

Prior to the war, about half the salt made on the Cape was used in the fishing industry. The remainder was shipped off by packets and coastal schooners. Still, the Cape Cod fishermen felt that President Jefferson was waging war on them. A minority of the people in New England were sympathetic to the British and feelings were mixed. Some states here had threatened secession but the embargo was repealed in 1809. This opened up trade with all nations except England and France. Since most of New

A deeply laden two masted schooner underway in the sound. These vessels could sail faster than most of the warships that were supposed to limit trade during the war years. *Photo by Bob Beattie.*

England's trade was with those two countries, the repeal offered little relief. James Madison succeeded Jefferson as President in 1809. He continued the economic warfare against Britain and this, along with further impressments of American seamen, precipitated the War of 1812.

The English were handicapped in this war because that nation was still in conflict with her interminable enemy, France. When compared to other wars of those times, the War of 1812 was brief. It did, however, succeed in gaining some rights and respect for Americans at home and abroad. There was some positive action by the U.S. Navy, notably the accomplishments of the *U.S.S. Constitution.* But around Cape Cod, Britain ruled the waters. This was a detriment to commerce because most all the Cape's business was carried by ships. An illicit coastal trade began and flourished for a time. One adventurous and enterprising captain from Falmouth ran the blockade to New York with a cargo of salt. He dyed his sails red so he could run at night without being detected. Most all communications with Boston were cut off by the English warships but many Barnstable Packets periodically ran the gauntlet in Massachusetts Bay, to maintain some semblance of trade. A large fleet of English warships patrolled here and exacted payments from towns who could little afford to pay. The H.M.S. *Spencer,* with her infamous Captain, Richard Raggett, was stationed in Provincetown Harbor.

During "Mr. Madison's War" the 52-gun *Spencer* sailed along the Bay shore and demanded the town of Brewster pay a ransom of $4,000. The British threatened to devastate the saltworks with cannon balls if the money was not forthcoming. The industry in that town was extensive, so they paid. It is interesting to note that during the 1976 United States Bicentennial celebration, the selectmen of Brewster sent a letter to London requesting that Britain repay the four thousand dollars, with interest. Queen Elizabeth II ignored the request and it is unfortunate that she did as the interest alone, if compounded, would have amounted in the millions of dollars for the town's treasury.

Along the Bay shores, other towns with a little backbone fared better. The people of the Cape were not fond of the English and many towns maintained a shore watch to detect any attempts at a landing. Captain Raggett demanded $1,000 from the town of Orleans and the Selectmen refused to pay. (A copy of Captain Raggett's letter appears in the appendix.) On December 19, 1814, a British force from the H.M.S. *Newcastle* landed at Rock Harbor and threatened to burn the saltworks. The local militia had been alerted and met them on the beach. Shots were fired and it was reported that two British soldiers were killed, while a few others were injured in the brief encounter. The redcoats left and did not return. It later became better known as the "Battle of Orleans." In 1855, the U.S. Congress granted a bounty of 160 acres to all surviving militiamen and pensions to many of the widows.

In Barnstable, Captain Raggett demanded a $6,000 ransom from Loring Crocker. His saltworks in the Common Fields covered a vast area, probably the largest on Cape Cod, and they were worth protecting. Mr. Crocker sent word to Boston for help and four cast-iron cannon were

Above: This historic marker stands at Rock Harbor in Orleans and locates the British landing during the War of 1812. The invaders were repulsed by the local militia. Below: The Old Powder House was used by the town of Harwich from 1770 to 1864. Gunpowder was stored for use by the local militia to protect the town in wartime. *Photos by William P. Quinn.*

Above: The front of the Barnstable County Courthouse with the two celebrated cannons, reportedly used during the War of 1812 to protect the harbor from invasion by the British. **Below:** A close-up view of one of the cannons mounted in a concrete carriage. It is still pointed towards Cape Cod Bay. *Photos by William P. Quinn.*

brought to Barnstable by ox-cart. He mounted them on the cliff to protect his property and the bluff worked. Some people, however, believed that it was the sand bar across Barnstable harbor that kept the British out, not the cannon. After the war was over, several young men in the town used these same cannon to celebrate the fourth of July holiday. If our earlier Cape historians are correct, two of these stalwart four-pounders are still visible in Barnstable today. They are mounted in concrete carriages in front of the Barnstable County Court House, still pointing towards the harbor, symbolically protecting the shire town while theoretically guarding the scales of justice.

On the south shore of Cape Cod, his majesty's brig *Nimrod* held forth in Nantucket and Vineyard Sounds. This ship carried out much the same marauding that Captain Raggett did in Cape Cod Bay. On January 28, 1814, notice was given to the town of Falmouth to release a sloop lying at the wharf and some brass four pound field pieces which had been furnished to the Falmouth Artillery company by the state. The classic answer from the local militia has been preserved in the town's history. Capt. Weston Jenkins replied: "Come and get them!" The Commander of the brig notified town officials that he would begin to fire at noon. Women and children were quickly evacuated. The bombardment lasted through the afternoon and into the evening. John Crocker said that eight cannon balls went through his house and saltworks. Several properties suffered damage including most all of the saltworks in the community. Today, there are a few round holes still left in some old Falmouth homes from this attack. The war ended on Christmas eve in 1814 when the Treaty of Ghent was signed in Belgium, but word did not arrive in the United States until some time later.

After the war, commerce began in earnest. The fighting had cost the Cape Cod businessmen a considerable amount in lost trade. It was then time to recoup for the unprofitable years of the conflict. During the war, many essential goods normally traded but then unavailable from England had to be manufactured in this country. Small industries were born and began to provide these commodities. Later, Congress enacted protective tariffs to shield these businesses. The manufacture of salt continued to be profitable because of the state bounty, government tariffs, and the improved technology employed.

There was another disaster for the salt-makers around Buzzards Bay. The gale of September 23, 1815 swept the exposed coastline of buildings, fences, trees, saltworks and all the ships caught in its path. We would probably refer to this storm as a hurricane today. The windstorm pushed the tide eight feet above normal and so much salt water was driven on land that it killed all of the vegetation, including many crops ready for harvest. All of the widespread saltworks along Buzzards Bay were carried away and torn to pieces. Some coasting vessels were carried so far inland that one came to rest in a forest, supported between trees. Most of the property facing the Bay was damaged heavily by the storm but the rest of Cape Cod escaped with little or no injury. During this period, the area around Buzzards Bay was still part of the town of Sandwich and was later to become the town of Bourne.

A strange phenomenon occurred in the year 1816. It was called the year without a summer, or the "mackerel year." A series of sun spots was believed by some to be the cause of snowfalls in June and July. There were other, more scientific explanations as well. In April, during the previous year, a mammoth eruption of one of the mountains in the southern Indonesian Island chain occurred and sent an estimated twenty-five cubic miles of debris into the high stratosphere. Mount Tambora, on the South Pacific island of Sumbawa, erupted violently killing an estimated ninety thousand people. The sound was heard nine hundred miles away. The sky was completely dark around the island for three days following the eruption. The dust cloud that spread out all over the world was blamed for the lack of summer in the United States in 1816. The adverse weather did not seriously affect Cape Cod but other regions of New England suffered greatly.

May of 1816 was not a warm month but the expected milder weather did not arrive in June. The New Bedford Mercury reported that the second week in June was very cold with high winds and frost. Above the Massachusetts border, Vermont, New Hampshire and Maine were experiencing cold weather and snowstorms. Many animals, wild and domestic, died in the cold weather. Gardens were destroyed by the frosts and there was concern for a harvest in the fall to carry people through the winter. There was one blessing during the mysterious weather. Some of the insects that attacked the crops were killed by the cold and it was several years before they returned. Birds which fed on these bugs had to find other food. Most of the damage was done in the three northern states. Connecticut, Rhode Island and Massachusetts did not suffer from snow or frost to any great extent but smaller crop yields were realized because of the unusual weather. Hay for cattle in northern New England sold at premium prices the following spring. The cost for other farm products was very high that year as well. Cape Cod did not suffer the extreme temperatures experienced in other parts of New England but there was less salt manufactured due to the lack of bright and warm sunlight. The fishing industry, however, saved the day for most. The "mackerel year" was so-called because fish supplemented the diet of those who had lost their harvests in the "year without a summer."

An unexplained malady occurred on the outer Cape during the first months of 1816. The epidemic swept through the towns from January to May and several persons died from what was described as: "an unusual sickness, the origin of which has never been satisfactorily ascertained" (Freeman's History). The worst area by far was the town of Eastham. The population there was approximately 800 people at the time. The disorder touched every family in town and seventy-two persons died. The disease affected all of the people in the towns from Brewster to Provincetown and the doctors could give no reason for the affliction. It is possible that the sickness may have been related to the volcano but not probable because people in the upper Cape were not bothered by the ailment.

The period following the War of 1812 was one of resurgence for the existing industries. More saltworks were built in every Cape town. Economic progress was widespread throughout all of Barnstable County as new factories for cotton, woolen cloth and shoes were begun in several towns. These were small establishments and significantly important to the overall economy but the maritime pursuits still dominated most of the industrial base on the Cape. Shipbuilding flourished as it never had before. In his book <u>Cape Cod</u> Henry C. Kittredge said: "Shipyards appeared like mushrooms beside every creek from Buzzards Bay to Provincetown." The dominance of the maritime industry over the Cape's economic development continued into the 1850's until the railroad arrived and completely altered the method of travel on the peninsula. These "Yankees," however, were not the type of people to change overnight. The transformation from sea to overland travel was gradual. The packets and coasters were sailing for several years following the coming of the railroad.

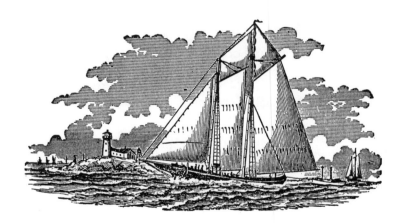

The noted disaster of October 3, 1841 is commemorated in Truro at an old burial ground. A marble shaft was erected with the names and ages of the 57 men lost in a tremendous storm. Seven fishing vessels from that town sank during the gale. The following ephitah was etched on the front of the stone:

SACRED to the memory of 57 citizens of Truro who were lost in seven vessels, which foundered at sea in the memorable gale of October 3, 1841.

"Then shall the dust return to the earth as it was; and the spirit shall return to the god who gave it."

"Man goeth to his long home and the mourners go about the streets."

Salt Taxes and

the Packet Boats

Chapter Four

An extraordinary age of industrial expansion took place in Europe during the fifteenth century. A similar period occurred in the United States during the first half of the nineteenth century. The economy of Cape Cod enlarged along with the rest of the country, nourished by the fishing and salt industries. The first fishing vessels were the single masted sloops and ketches. These slower boats were later replaced by the two-masted schooners. The bigger ships could carry larger cargoes and sail faster. They journeyed south to the West Indies, where they traded their salt-fish cargo to feed the slaves that worked in the cane fields. The return cargoes consisted of sugar, molasses, cotton, salt and rum.

In the year 1837, codfish was plentiful. Significant modifications in fishing techniques had been adopted and larger catches were realized. The boats of Barnstable County brought in 134,658 quintals of cod during the year. The figures for the individual towns were important: Provincetown (51,400), Orleans (20,000), Truro (16,520), Harwich (10,000), Chatham (15,500), Wellfleet (3,100), Yarmouth (4,300), Sandwich (2,100), Eastham (1,200), Barnstable (267) and Brewster (800). The relative importance of this industry to the economic health of Cape Cod need not be under-estimated. There was a large market for salt to support these fisheries and most of it was manufactured locally. The inter-dependent industries in Barnstable County enjoyed continued growth too but there were changes in the offing after the middle of the century.

Above: Coastal schooners were frequently wrecked on the backside of Cape Cod. The schooner *Plymouth Rock* came aground, with a load of lumber, at Peaked Hill Bars in Provincetown on April 11, 1888. *Photo courtesy of Cape Cod Photos, Orleans, Mass.* **Below:** When a total wreck occurs in the winter, the abandoned hull becomes a playground in the summer. Due to the lack of fuel on Cape Cod, these vessels were often cut apart for firewood by the local residents. *Photo from the Author's collection.*

The success of the fishing industry did not come without a cost. Early maritime records reveal stories of violent weather with terrible storms which invariably took a considerable toll in ships and human life. One of these storms wrecked scores of vessels in 1837 and 78 men from Cape Cod perished. But by far, one of the greatest losses in the annals occurred when a late fall hurricane swept up the east coast on October 2, 1841 and wrecked the Cape's fishing fleet on Georges Bank. The storm raged for four days before it abated. The hardest hit town on Cape Cod was Truro. This town lost seven fishing vessels and fifty-seven sailors. Most of the men were young but the disaster left 19 widows and 39 children without fathers. The town went into mourning and a fund was set up to aid the families of the men lost in the storm.

One other town, Dennis, lost 22 of her men at the same time. The total for the entire Cape, was 14 vessels and 87 men. There were several wrecks along the back shore of the Cape in addition to the ones lost at sea. The high winds damaged buildings and knocked down large trees. Crops not yet harvested were ruined and in some areas, the winds uprooted fences. Additional damage was done along the bay shores as many wharves were broken apart. Several tons of salt hay which had been cut and stacked in the marshes was carried off by the high tides and lost. The damage to the saltworks along the coastline was substantial. The salt vats that sustained injury in the storm were not rebuilt. The bank panic of 1837 had brought on a depression in this country which continued for several years. The gale of 1841 exacerbated the already weakened economy on Cape Cod.

Maritime commerce around New England was, in some seasons, a gamble for those involved in shipping. It was, frequently, very hazardous to venture forth on coastal waters carrying cargo to and from distant ports. There were no official weather forecasts and northeast storms came, sometimes without warning, and cast ships ashore in a helter-skelter pattern. During the winter, after a stiff nor'easter, one could often see an intermittent picket fence of masts from ships grounded along the backside. The waters around Cape Cod were dubbed the "Graveyard of ships" by the captains of vessels lost here. During the great gale of February 22nd, 1802

The first lighthouse on Cape Cod was at the Highlands at Truro and its beacon was flashed to sea for the first time in 1797. It is the largest lighthouse on Cape Cod and as it nears the 200th anniversary the erosion of the cliff it stands on threatens to topple the lighthouse into the sea. There are present day efforts to raise funds to save the light. *Photo by Henry K. Cummings.*

three East India ships, the *Volusia,* Captain Samuel Cook, the *Ulysses,* Captain James Cook, and the *Brutus,* Captain William Brown, were wrecked near Peaked Hill Bars. The disaster brought with it a heavy loss of life from the three vessels. The dollar amount of loss was listed as $200,000 at the time.

Shipwrecks were, however, another part of the Cape economy. When vessels came ashore during storms, the crews were frequently lost. After the weather cleared, the wrecked hulls often lay in the sands with cargoes intact. The salvage of these cargoes was an extra source of income for many Cape Codders. This practice became a profitable business during the 19th century. At Monomoy Point, a small fishing village gradually grew into a settlement of wreckers. These men made a good living from the disasters on the outer beaches off Chatham, Monomoy and from the shoals south of Cape Cod. Ships carrying diverse cargoes were rich sources for the wreckers and salvagers, but not salt. If a ship with a cargo of salt were sunk off Cape Cod, it would invariably lie on the bottom for a couple of weeks until the salt disolved. Later, the wooden hull would float to the surface, minus her cargo, and if possible, the vessel was salvaged.

When the Federal Government began to erect lighthouses along the coast, Cape wreckers fought unsuccessfully against the proposed navigational improvements. These early lights were fueled by sperm oil from whales. The first lighthouse erected on Cape Cod was at Truro in 1797. This was called Highland Light. Other lighthouses were erected at Chatham in 1806; Race Point at Provincetown in 1816; Billingsgate Island off Wellfleet in 1822; Monomoy Point off Chatham in 1823; Long Point at Provincetown in 1826; Nobska Point at Woods Hole in 1828; Sandy Neck at Barnstable in 1836 and the controversial three sisters lights on the outer shores of Eastham in 1838. The reason for the contention was the opinions by many that one light could do the work of three at much less cost. The aids to navigation did help to reduce the shipwrecks around Cape Cod but not completely. The reduction in the number of these wrecks, however, was welcome news for businessmen engaged in maritime commerce.

With the success of the saltworks industry, it was inevitable that the

This photograph was taken in Provincetown in the later part of the nineteenth century. This was the Whaling Brig *D.A. Small* up on the ways for repairs. The whaling industry contributed to the Cape Cod economy during the 18th and 19th centuries. *Photograph by Henry K. Cummings.*

government would levy taxes. In those towns where salt manufacturing took place, each owner of salt vats was assessed by the superficial foot. In 1829, the Town of Chatham listed in the Assessor's Valuation, 143,665 feet of saltworks. The value placed on the works was $57,291. The collection of taxes today covers a multitude of items and it was no different in former days. The other properties and assets on the Chatham assessors list in 1829 were: number of Grist Mills (7), number of barns (144), number of tons of vessels, five tons and upwards (3,467), number of acres of tillage land (325), number of acres of pasture land (2,485), number of horses over one year old (135) and number of acres of unimproved land (1,310).

The revised state laws were enacted in 1829. The manufacturing had begun in the later part of the eighteenth century and why the Massachusetts Legislature waited so long to levy taxes was not revealed in the early records. Of the many reasons considered, one might be that the lawmakers declined to pass a tax law when the industry began in order to stimulate the slow post-war economy in the Bay State. They had originally paid a bounty on each bushel of salt manufactured in the state by evaporation of sea water. The revised statutes passed on November 4, 1835 for the Commonwealth of Massachusetts were as follows:

Chapter 28. Sect. 192 of the General Laws. "There shall be three inspectors general of salt manufactured in this state, who shall be well skilled in the manufacture; one for the counties of Barnstable and Duke's county; one for the county of Bristol; and one for the remaining counties; and they shall give bond, with sufficient sureties, to the treasurer of the Commonwealth, in the penal sum of two thousand dollars."

Section 193 described the duties of deputy inspectors: a number sufficient to execute the provisions of law and provide bonds for them to carry out their inspections. Section 194 set the fees: "The inspectors general, or their deputies, shall receive of the manufacturer of salt, for their services, each time when said services shall be required and rendered, twenty cents upon every ten thousand superficial feet of salt works with covers, and half of that sum, when the works in which they may so inspect have no covers, and at the same rate for a greater or smaller number of feet; provided, however, that when the saltworks, in which said salt is to be inspected, are of the brush work construction, they shall be entitled to receive of the manufacturer of salt for their services aforesaid twenty cents for every one thousand superficial feet of salt vats, in which they may so inspect, and at the same rate for a greater or smaller number of feet."

Section 195 set down the Inspectors' proportion of the deputies' fees and appointed a deputy in each town. Section 196 laid down the manner of inspection: "When any manufacturer shall be prepared to remove any salt from his vats, he shall, before removing the same, apply to the inspector, within whose limits the salt works may be situated, to inspect the same, and said inspector shall proceed to inspect such salt before it shall be removed from the vats; and if in his judgment it be necessary in order to ascertain its quality, he shall cause the impure brine, which may be in the vats with the salt to be inspected, to be drawn off, and after having caused the salt in said vats to be broken up, he shall cause such vats to be supplied with a sufficient quantity of new brine, to purify said salt and enable him to ascertain the quality thereof; and said new brine shall remain in said vats not less than twenty four hours, and if, after this process, the inspector shall approve the quality of the salt so inspected, he shall forthwith give to the manufacturer a written or printed permit to remove said salt."

Sections 197 and 198 set forth the duties of the manufacturer and penalties on inspectors for unreasonable delays in inspections. These laws would not seem to put undue hardships on the manufacturers of salt. It is likely that the deputies could schedule daily inspections at their own convenience because the evaporation process took three weeks to complete. The men appointed as inspectors were undoubtedly political appointments, reserved for friends and loyal backers. The other men, appointed as deputy inspectors, were probably saltmakers themselves as the requirements included being "well skilled in the manufacture." The men who were employed only worked six months a year but they, no doubt, had saltworks of their own. Massachusetts, however, did not enjoy the benefits of a bountiful income from this industry. It was at this time, that the business had begun its decline because of foreign competition after the removal of tariffs by Congress and the discovery of salt mines elsewhere in this country.

There were, sometimes, instances where politics affected the salt inspectors. The duties were not always carried out in the manner set down by law. With the limited communications available in those days, it is a wonder that more graft and corruption did not take place. An advertisement appeared in the Barnstable Patriot on November 21, 1832 as a warning to those who strayed from their proper actions:

"To the Manufacturer's and Inspectors of Salt in the Counties of Barnstable and Duke's.

"The Inspector General gives notice, that, in future, all applications for, and discharges of, Inspectors, must be made in the months of December, January and February; otherwise the applications will not be complied with - except where vacancies occur by death or removal.

"The Inspectors are hereby notified - that they have permission, if for their accommodation, to make their returns of Inspection as follows, viz: To Samuel P. Crosswell, Esq. Falmouth - Ebenezer Bacon, Esq. County Treasurer, Barnstable - Capt. Samuel Freeman, Jr., Eastham - John Kenney, Esq. Truro, and to the subscriber in Brewster. The Inspectors of Dukes County may make their returns to Capt. Presbury Norton, of Tisbury, who will forward them to Falmouth, as before directed.

"The Inspector General regrets the necessity of thus publicly noticing the inattention of some Inspectors to the obligation of their oaths, as to the time of making their returns, (December 15th annually) notwithstanding the accommodating provision, and ample time allowed for that purpose. The consequence is great inconvenience.

"But there is another delinquency, more serious to notice, viz: - two instances, in the 1831, of no return at all. The conclusion is, that no Inspection has been made in said Districts; - of course the law disregarded entirely. It is to be hoped that this hint, will produce an immediate and satisfactory explanation, and prevent further investigation of the subject.

"ELIJAH COBB, Inspector General, Brewster, Nov. 17, 1831."

This is an artist's conception of the typical Packet vessel of the 18th and 19th centuries. The single masted sloop could carry a large cargo in her hold and several people in the roomy cabin on deck. *Drawing by Paul C. Morris, Nantucket, Mass.*

THE PACKET BOATS

The local packet boats added a most interesting era to the Cape's maritime history. The early coastal trading vessels around Cape Cod dated back before the middle of the eighteenth century. No one knows just when the packets started, probably around the beginning of the 19th century but there is no fixed date. The dictionary describes the packet as "A vessel conveying dispatches, mails, passengers and goods, and having fixed sailing days." There are a great many local legends as to when they started on the Cape. The story about an Eastham farmer has been told and retold and no doubt embellished as it was passed along but it supports most of the theories carried through by many generations. This version relates that the man had a cargo of onions to be taken to the market in Boston. He engaged a fishing vessel for this purpose and then decided to go along and oversee the deal himself. His wife had some shopping to do in the city and wanted to accompany her husband. Soon another friend joined him for the trip. Later, a neighbor wanted to know why the farmer was leaving on a fishing boat. There were no telephones in those days but it didn't take long for the word to get around and quickly, the Captain had other passengers with business in Boston. It seemed like a good idea and soon, other captains found the concept to have possibilities.

The packets maintained an erratic schedule. Usually the captain would sail as close to the posted time as possible but, as sailboats need a favorable wind, the weather was the deciding factor controlling the departure and arrival times. Most captains, however, when asked when the boat would sail replied: "We might leave when the hold is full." For some, it was extra revenue but for others, the business of carrying freight and passengers became more lucrative than fishing, and, with much less risk. It is, perhaps, interesting to note that in modern times, the captain of such a vessel would not be able to carry on his business. Today's Coast Guard rules for such boats would prohibit the carrying of passengers. The same

A Rock Harbor packet vessel grounded out on the flats at low tide at Orleans. At this location, the passengers could board without getting their feet wet, then wait for the tide to come in and float the schooner. These vessels were engaged in coastal trading and they made substantial profits for their owners. *Photo courtesy of the Orleans Historical Society.*

regulations would not allow him leave port without several thousand dollars worth of special navigational and communications equipment. But the early Cape Cod packet captains needed none of these. They had an uncanny sixth sense of direction and, with compass and lead-line, could set their course for Boston with no need from any other navigational aids. Another attribute possessed by those early captains was a keen eye for the weather. They usually knew when a storm was due and could carry on their business accordingly.

Following the war of 1812, packet vessels were carrying full loads of goods and passengers back and forth to Boston, from nearly every town on Cape Cod, at almost any time of the year. There were usually several hogsheads of salt included in these cargoes. There were other commodities shipped off Cape. These included onions, rye and flax. Full cargoes of firewood were loaded at Sandwich. Many vessels were built for passenger comforts. With these improvements, new vessels accommodated their guests in pleasant cabins. Meals were served to seasoned travelers while the first timers usually hugged the rails until they got their sea legs. In Truro, opulence and pleasure began to appear in Cape Cod society. The packet schooner *Postboy* was renowned for her elegant appointments. Her cabins were finished in birds-eye maple and mahogany with silk drapes. Her crew developed their social skills among the passengers and the twenty-five cent meal became an epicurean's delight served by a gracious steward. The packets carried a varied list of passengers. The deep water sailing captain used the packet boat to return home after a long overseas voyage. Often his wife would travel to the city to meet her husband and they would come home together. A closer look into that form of travel was outlined in Deyo's History, published in 1890:

"The mode of travel by the packets was much better adapted to the promotion of sociability and the cultivation of acquaintanceship than our present rapid transit by rail. With twenty-five to fifty persons crowded into the cabins and upon the decks of a small schooner, as was often the case, there was frequent occasion to exercise the graces of courtesy, self-forgetfulness and consideration for the convenience of others. Men and women, thrown together under such circumstances, soon became sociable and communicative. All sorts of topics were discussed, from original sin to the price of codfish. Experiences were related and results compared. When these resources were exhausted recourse was had to amusements, and not unfrequently the younger and less rigid of the passengers would perhaps resort to a game of checkers, or a quiet game of 'old sledge,' down in the hold or the forecastle. Travel by packet was a great leveler of social distinctions - the squire, the village storekeeper, the minister or the doctor being constrained to take up with the same fare as their more humble neighbors, upon whom they were obliged to depend for some degree of deference or courtesy. On the other hand, these important personages often felt impelled to exercise a degree of condescension to those with whom they were thrown in such intimate relations."

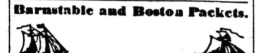

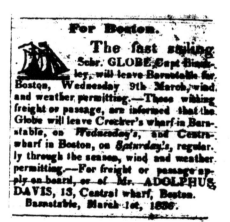

Ads for Packet Schooners were listed in the weekly papers in Barnstable County. The vessels usually made a fast passage to and from Boston and were the preferred mode of travel for Cape Codders.

A trip on the packet in the mid nineteenth century was, no doubt, viewed differently for those traveling to Boston from Cape Cod. To the young adult couple, a touch of romance was never avoided while alone, near the forward deck, on a bright moonlit night with a quartering breeze and the bow wave breaking in front of the stem with a gentle splash. The scene had the potential for varied results. To the children, lucky enough to be included on the journey, the possibilities were limitless. The vessel, indeed, must have seemed enormous. A run around the deck houses was probably great fun just before sailing. Most of the boisterous behavior, however was probably held in check by the adults. To the older generation, it was looked upon as a pleasant trip in good weather. But even in squally conditions, the vessel, underway with greater speed and taught lines, provided some unforgetable sailing. In the days before the automobile, a ride aboard a schooner, on a broad reach, making ten or eleven knots must have been exciting.

Most of the passengers gathered in the early afternoon on the pier. They boarded the schooner just after the cargo was loaded into the holds, while keeping an eye cocked at the weather. Just after getting underway, a good dinner was usually served. The menu included: Clam chowder, salt fish, baked potatoes, huckleberry duff and coffee. This was topped off with hot gingerbread for dessert. The meal usually cost a quarter and was welcome by all except those with queasy stomachs.

Departure time was in the late afternoon, depending on the tides and winds. When the ship was well off shore, the wind increased, unaffected by the hills and valleys of the land. The schooner's decks canted gracefully as the bow pointed north. Most of the passage occurred during the night hours except when light winds becalmed the vessel. There were times when the trip could take two or three days if calm conditions persisted. During a normal passage, early risers could catch a glimpse of Minot's Ledge light, just before the vessel turned to the westward around Point Allerton. Near the end of the voyage, the packet schooner passed Boston Light and under reduced sails made her way to the pier. The vessel then tied up at the T-Wharf to unload her passengers and cargo early in the day.

When conditions were right, the packet Captains would often race their boats in competition with each other on the trip to Boston. There were some lively wagers made and quite often a few dollars would change hands when the vessels reached the city. These ships carried romantic names like *Winged Hunter, Eagle Flight* and *Emerald.* The packets were most always the same type of vessel, the two masted schooner of one hundred tons or less.

The Chatham Stage ran until 1872 until the trains took over carrying the mail and passengers. Photo courtesy of the *Harwich Historical Society.*

Stagecoach travel was not as popular with Cape Codders as the packets. The journey to Boston over land was never pleasant. Dusty, rough roads and the fording of streams tended to dissuade even the most hardy traveler. The rudimentary trails between the Cape and Boston were not as well maintained as the Post Roads in the rest of the country and surface travel was never attempted except as a last resort. Overland by stage was sometimes a gamble because stormy weather caused floods and roads became impassable. The coach was never sealed against the weather and in the winter, the cold was almost unbearable. Another factor was the disposition of the driver under these conditions. He sometimes blamed his very existance on the passengers who suffered through the whole ordeal. It was a tough job at any time let alone in bad weather. Travel by stage improved in 1827 when the Concord Coach replaced the covered wagons and conditions were much better for the passengers but still at the snails pace of six miles per hour. Unlike the packet vessels, which depended on the wind, under optimum conditions, the coach could maintain some semblence of a schedule along the roads.

The boats, however, were most always reliable. It was only a one or two day trip depending on the weather and wind direction. A fair wind could shorten the voyage to eight hours or less. The return of the packet to Cape Cod was eagerly awaited by all. Signals on high hills alerted the residents of the lower Cape towns when the boats were in sight. There is some high land in Dennis called Signal Hill. It was named for a tall mast that once stood there to announce the arrival or departure of a vessel. The packets did a good business until the 1850's when the first rail lines were completed to Cape Cod. But old habits are hard to change and the boats continued in business. On Tuesday, March 6, 1860, an advertisement appeared in the Barnstable Patriot for the packet schooner *Mail,* Capt. A. H. Young, for Boston. The vessel left every Wednesday from Maraspin's Wharf in Barnstable and every Saturday from Boston's India Wharf, (in the immediate vicinity of Norris & Baxter's Saloon). "Freights will be taken on the most reasonable terms."

On August 17, 1807, an event took place on the Hudson River in New York that was to effect a marked change in future maritime travel. Robert Fulton made the first practical steamboat trip from New York City to Albany. The trip took thirty-two hours to complete but the birth of steam power had come upon the nation. This event was to have an adverse affect on the saltworks of Cape Cod in later years. In order to compete with the railroad, steamboats were later employed on the Cape to Boston run but even they could not survive and by 1870, regular train schedules were being maintained. The change was gradual, however, and a few sailing packets were still carrying freight into the early 1900's.

The 1820's were the years of greatest expansion for the saltworks on Cape Cod. The various histories give interesting descriptions of the saltworks along the shores. Deyo's History, published in 1890, carried several notable anecdotes:

"Salt-mills and saltworks extended along the Provincetown shore from one end of the town to another, giving to the town a picturesque appearance, which is not wholly lost in the early wood cuts of the town that are still preserved in rare copies of the gazetteers of Massachusetts."

"Most of the Falmouth salt found a ready market at home, as the fishing fleet, hundreds of vessels, would put in here in the spring and fill their holds with salt before starting for the Banks. The salt was also used in Falmouth homes, and Mr. Hewins remembers how it was one of his boyhood tasks to get the mortar and pestle and grind up salt for the family table."

An illustration of a Cape Cod saltworks in the early 1800's. One of the buildings may be a storage building and the other might be a drying room for salt. A typical scene of the era. *Reproduced from Deyo's History of Barnstable County, 1890.*

"The earliest industry of the village of Chatham, always excepting fishing, was the manufacture of salt, which soon after 1800 received considerable attention. These works, interspersed with flakes for drying fish, nearly covered the shore from the Sears' plant northeast of the village, southerly to the lights, around the shores of both ponds, and the rivers connecting them with the harbor."

By 1837 the saltworks business had reached its zenith. A list was published of all the Cape Cod towns and their numbers were impressive:

Barnstable: ..... 34 establishments producing 27,125 bushels annually.
Brewster: .... 60 establishments producing 34,500 bushels annually.
Chatham: .... 80 establishments producing 27,400 bushels annually.
Dennis: .... 114 establishments producing 52,200 bushels annually.
Eastham: .... 54 establishments producing 22,370 bushels annually.
Falmouth: .... 42 establishments producing 24,500 bushels annually.
Harwich: .... 8 establishments producing 8,000 bushels annually.
Orleans: .... 50 establishments producing 21,780 bushels annually.
Provincetown: 78 establishments producing 48,960 bushels annually.
Sandwich: .... 8 establishments producing 2,670 bushels annually.
Truro: .... 39 establishments producing 17,490 bushels annually.
Wellfleet: .... 39 establishments producing 10,000 bushels annually.
Yarmouth: ..... 52 establishments producing 365,200 bushels annually.

The figures as listed show 658 establishments producing a total of 662,195 bushels of salt, or over twenty-six thousand tons. The Cape Codders were making a substantial living on their salt and fishing industries. The way of life here was changing rapidly and mostly for the better. Salt was not the only commodity making money in those early days. One of the more profitable items came out of Nantucket. An article in the Nantucket Inquirer in May, 1845 revealed the value of whale oil:

"Nantucket, Mass. The ship Ohio, which recently arrived at the port of Nantucket, from the Pacific Ocean, has turned out on the wharf, 2,810 barrels of sperm oil, and has sold on the voyage, about 80 barrels sperm and shale, making 2,890 barrels in all, valued at about eighty-one thousand dollars. The Potomac has also turned out on the wharf 2,354 barrels of sperm oil, and has sold on the voyage 90 barrels sperm, making 2,444 barrels in all, valued at about sixty-nine thousand dollars. The Nantucket also is at the bar, with about 1,330 barrels sperm (including oil sent home) 1,300 do whale, and 13,000 lbs. bone, valued at about fifty-six thousand dollars. This makes an aggregate of two hundred and six thousand dollars for three ships. Can our "Off Island" brethren beat this?"

The whale fisheries had a significant influence in the history of the United States beginning in the seventeenth century and extending into the early 1900's. This practice has faded into the past with today's technology and alternate sources of energy. Museums at Nantucket and New Bedford, Massachusetts contain large collections of memorabilia telling the epic story of the whaling days. *Drawing by Paul C. Morris, Nantucket, Massachusetts.*

The New Bedford and Nantucket whaling fleet were profitable enterprises. In this reproduction of a painting, the whaleship *Kutusoff* is depicted cutting up a whale. *Painting by Benjamin Russell of New Bedford.*

The Jonathan Young Windmill of Orleans in the 1890's. One of the oldest on Cape Cod, built circa 1720, in South Orleans and moved to the center of town in 1850's. The mill was purchased by a retired sea captain and moved to Hyannisport in 1897. The structure was returned to Orleans in 1983 and restored. It now stands, overlooking the Town Cove, in a two-acre park. The mill is open to the public in the summer months. *Photo by H. K. Cummings.*

The Diverse Cape Cod Industries

Chapter Five

The earliest mechanical industry on Cape Cod was the gristmill. Two types of natural energy were used, water and wind. There were a few water driven mills of note but at one time there were thirty-nine operating windmills on Cape Cod. These were round or octagonal buildings with huge exterior fan-like arms turning on a center shaft and usually situated on a high hill to catch the maximum winds. Because the only transportation at that time for the average person was by horse and buggy, the windmills had to be located away from roads so as not to frighten the horses. The gristmill should not to be confused with the smaller salt-mills set up on a framework base to pump sea water for the saltworks. Most of the large Cape windmills were used for grinding grain but a few were used in the salt industry to produce a finer grain salt for table use. The East Mill in Orleans began as a salt grinding mill. This mill has been preserved and is located at the Heritage Plantation in Sandwich. It is not known whether any of the water driven mills was used to process salt.

There was one windmill on Cape Cod for which a patent was issued, signed by President James Monroe, and was supposed to cut and polish stone. Other signatures on the document were John Quincy Adams, Secretary of State and William Wirt as Attorney-General. There is very little information available as to the amount of work done by this mill or whether it was used for other purposes.

Corn was the major crop in that era and the kernels were difficult

Above: The Judah Baker windmill was built at Dennis in 1791. It was moved to South Yarmouth in 1866. One of the salt-mills can be seen on the left hand side of the photograh. **Below:** Perhaps the most famous mill on Cape Cod was the Farris Windmill at West Yarmouth. It was considered to be the oldest mill on the Cape, built sometime in the middle of the seventeenth century. The mill remained in Yarmouth until the mid 1930's when it was moved to Dearborn, Michigan, and became part of the Ford Museum of Americana.

to grind by hand. It was a tedious chore and the amount obtained by this method was minimal. The Pilgrims remembered the windmills in Holland and the word spread for millwrights who could build and maintain a windmill. Man had learned early the art of harnessing the forces of nature to do the hard work. The Cape windmills ground corn for Johnny-cake meal. This commodity helped sustain the entire community and even served as the basis of the local money as the values were measured in bushels of corn instead of currency of which there was little. Water mills preceeded windmills, yet on the Cape there was little water power but lots of wind. Another factor was that windmills never froze up in the winter. Operations of the water powered mills were limited to the milder months whereas the windmills could operate anytime the wind was right; providing the temperature was not too cold as there was no way to heat the interior of the windmills without the danger of fire. In the 1600's the millwrights began to erect their mills.

The picturesque structures had other attributes. Beside their contributions to the local scenery, sailors at sea used the Cape Cod windmills and lighthouses as landmarks for navigation. Sometimes the millers were known as "dry land sailors" because they had to set and reef canvas sails on the windvanes. When modern technology retired the old wind powered mills, some were moved to decorate estates of the well-to-do around Cape Cod while still others were saved for historic exhibits. The longevity of the windmills was due to the fact that their frames and machinery were built, in most cases, of the toughest native oak. In modern days, old mills that remain on the Cape still stand rigid against nature without any signs of weakness in their time worn frames.

The post and beam framework of a windmill was held together by wooden pegs. This was important as the stresses, resulting from the energy transfered inside while the mill was running were enormous. The huge blades in front of the octagonal building turned a main shaft which was geared to the grinding stones. But it was a dangerous occupation in a good fresh wind. Few if any nails were used although local blacksmiths did supply some iron bolts and straps to hold the vital parts of the structure in place where wooden pegs could not. During the milling process, with a good twelve to twenty mile-an-hour wind, the entire building would shake and vibrate. The structure itself was somewhat flexible in order to withstand these motions but the sound emanating from inside was sometimes unsettling to those not familiar with the operations.

Occasionally there were accidents to the old mills. Cape Cod winds were not predictable and if there was an unexpected increase in speed, which was not uncommon, the mill frequently ran out of control. The usual result was a fire from the uncontrolled friction and total loss of the building. There were no fire departments to call in the 18th century. A careful miller always had enough help nearby to keep the operations under control. Today there are six windmills and three water powered mills preserved as historic exhibits on Cape Cod and are, probably, the most photographed antique structures in New England. All the others have succumbed to the march of time. One old mill in Truro was used as a target for gunnery practice by British vessels in the War of 1812. There is an ancient windmill on Nantucket Island, built from the timbers of wrecked ships. This mill still runs and it grinds corn meal which is sold to tourists during the summer months. Henry David Thoreau came to Cape Cod in 1849 and saw the windmills scattered around the countryside. In his book <u>Cape Cod</u> he described his thoughts about these strange structures:

"The most foreign and picturesque structures on the Cape, to an inlander, not excepting the saltworks, are the windmills, - gray-looking, octagonal towers, with long timbers slanting to the ground in the rear, and there resting on a cartwheel, by which their fans are turned round to face the wind. These appeared also to serve in some measure for props against its force. A great circular rut was worn around the building by the wheel. The neighbors who assemble to turn the mill to the wind are likely to know which way it blows, without a weather-cock. They looked loose and slightly locomotive, like huge wounded birds, trailing a wing or a leg, and reminded one of the pictures of the Netherlands.

"Being on elevated ground, and high in themselves, they serve as landmarks, - for there are no tall trees, or other objects commonly, which can be seen at a distance in the horizon; though the outline of the land itself is so firm and distinct, that an insignificant cone, or even precipice of sand, is visible at a great distance from over the sea. Sailors making the land commonly steer either by the wind mills, or the meeting-houses. In the country, we are obliged to steer by the meeting-houses alone. Yet the meeting-house is a kind of wind mill, which runs one day in seven, turned either by the winds of doctrine or public opinion, or more rarely by the winds of Heaven, where another sort of grist is ground, of which, if it be not all bran or musty, if it be not *plaster,* we trust to make bread of life."

Above: One of the oldest water mills on Cape Cod is Dexter's Grist Mill in Sandwich. The structure was built in 1654 and serves today as a major tourist attraction in the town. **Below:** Another popular mill for visitors is in Brewster at Stoney Brook Mill. Situated on a herring run, it is a busy spot during the spring. This mill is open during the summer months and still grinds corn meal for sale to visitors. *Photos by William P. Quinn.*

Some water mills have survived to the present day. One, the Dexter Grist mill in Sandwich was built by Thomas Dexter in 1654 and was the first of its kind on the Cape. A large wheel with mechanical gears inside, powered by water from inland ponds dropping slowly and silently towards the sea through a brook rich with herring every spring. This mill has served several masters at various callings over the ages and is currently a tourist attraction; but still grinding corn meal. Another example of water power is at Brewster on Stoney Brook Road where summer visitors can view with fascination the operation of an antique mill on a few selected weekday afternoons. Stone ground corn meal is sold to visitors and the consensus is that it makes delicious muffins. This mill was originally built in 1873 and is now a museum owned by the Town of Brewster.

On Route 28 in West Yarmouth today, the Baxter Mill still stands. Built in 1710 by John and Shubel Baxter, this mill ran for almost two hundred years and only the changing times retired this jewel of Cape Cod's historic past. After it ceased to grind grain, the building served several different purposes but in 1961 it was restored to working condition with a metal turbine underneath the building to convert falling water to mechanical power. In 1989 the mill was again renovated and is now open to the public in the afternoon during the summer months. This mill is owned by the town of Yarmouth.

There is evidence around the Cape shorelines that tidewater mills were in operation in the mid 17th to early 18th century. In Orleans the early histories report three such mills, one at Arey's pond, another at Sparrow's pond and there are remains of a stone foundation across the entrance to Mill pond in the Tonset area that are still visible today. This area was the location of one of the large saltworks in Orleans. Other records show that a tidewater mill operated at the Salt Pond in Eastham. There were other mills of this type in many of the estuaries all over Cape Cod. The operation was quite simple. A large salt-pond was utilized where a small entrance was breeched with a dam. As the tide came in, the gates were opened. At high tide, the gates were closed. The mill was situated on top of the dam with a water wheel to utilize the power created by the falling tide. The operations

Above: An old photograph at Sandwich of the glass works. The plant no longer exists today but the products made there are considered to be one of the finest types of glassware. Today, there is a Museum in the town holding a large collection of "Sandwich Glass." *Photo by H. K. Cummings.* **Below:** This is a copy of a painting by Ben Neill at the Sandwich Glass Museum of the steamer *Acorn*. The steamer is pictured at the wharf in Sandwich. In the foreground is a horse drawn cart filled with barrels of glass ready for loading. The horse railway over the marshes was constructed by Deming Jarves in 1833 to solve the problem of transporting supplies and glass from the factory site to deeper water where vessels could tie up.

of these mills would have to be carried out during the milder months of the year.

One of the more enterprising manufacturing industries on Cape Cod was the Boston and Sandwich Glass Company in Sandwich. The business was founded in 1826 by Deming Jarves. But it wasn't the Cape Cod sand that brought the glass factory here, it was the vast acreage of hardwood forests destined to be used as fuel in the glass furnaces. The sand was shipped in from New Jersey. Sandwich became a factory community, employing at one time five hundred skilled men, manufacturing what was described as a "superior product." New and unique pieces of colored glass were featured and its popularity caused the company to expand their work force and markets. The Cape plant turned out "special manufactured pieces" for a distinguished clientele the world over. Some of the unique pieces created were candlesticks, cup plates, lamps and lampshades, decanters, bowls, cruets, doorknobs, and various types of cut-glass. The colors featured were amber, blue, green, opalescent, purple and ruby.

The plant operated successfully for sixty years until labor problems and a strike shut it down in 1887. In the middle of the 19th century it was a 600,000 dollar a year business. Deming Jarves even had his own coastal schooner. The sloop *Polly* maintained a rigorous schedule between Sandwich and Boston. It was not known if any salt was carried aboard the sloop but probably a full load of glass was in the hold on every trip. Later, after the railroad came to Cape Cod, what were described as "exorbitant freight rates" caused Deming Jarves to build his own steamboat. The *Acorn*, built in 1854, carried barrels of glass products as well as passengers to and from Boston until the freight rates moderated on the railroad.

In the present era, we are battling with the problems of efficiency and the environment. An article appeared an 1840 edition of the Yarmouth Register describing the performance of the Sandwich Glass factory during that period.

"In the management of the concerns of the Boston and Sandwich Glass Company, the greatest order is maintained, and in every department

Above: The "Drummer" of the 1890's with his horse and wagon. Before the days of automobiles, horse powered vehicles were rated at one. It appears that this photograph was made in the winter months with snow on the ground. The man had on a heavy winter coat as he posed with his dapple gray horse while on his rounds selling Wood's Spices. Door to door salesmen were common in the nineteenth century selling practically everything needed in the home. *Photo by H. K. Cummings.*
Below: Another small Cape Cod industry was ice. The cakes were cut from frozen ponds in the winter and stored in sheds insulated with hay and wood shavings. About half of the ice was still solid when summer came and it was sold to householders in small pieces for ice-boxes to keep food cold. *Photo from the collection of Matthews C. Hallet, Yarmouthport, Mass.*

of its business the strictest economy in the use of materials and in the application of labor and mechanical power is observable. Nothing is lost. Everything is applied to some use. The fire for the steam-engine is kept up with chips and refuse coal, and the heat is conveyed in iron pipes under pans filled with sea water, for the manufacture of salt. The heated air, which by this arrangement is saved, evaporates water sufficient to make ten bushels of salt per day. All the ashes made in the establishment are collected and leached, and the lye boiled down to potash."

This is an interesting side light in the study of the manufacture of salt. An inquiry into the records of the Boston and Sandwich Glass Works at the Sandwich Glass Museum revealed that waste heat from the furnaces was used to evaporate sea water and make salt. Each furnace generated twenty-three hundred degrees. This would seem ample to evaporate 3,500 gallons of sea water and make ten bushels of salt. The early records in the Museum, however, are unclear about this operation. Deming Jarves was the consummate entrepreneur and many of his supplemental operations were carried out to increase profits for the business. The Boston and Sandwich Glass Works Board of Directors held their meetings in Boston and knowledge of the operations at the factory were mostly by official reports.

There were other land industries on Cape Cod but none as large as the Sandwich Glass Factory. An early fulling mill for woolen cloth operated in Marstons Mills in Barnstable. After the War of 1812, a cotton spinning mill was producing in Sandwich for a short time. Another company on the lower Cape made cotton shirting for a while. In Falmouth, two woolen mills operated successfully during the period and they tried to manufacture silk at one time but not on a large scale. Shoemaking was practiced in almost every town on the Cape but the effort was not in a central location. The work was piecemeal and scattered around in homes and small shops. In Falmouth some shoe manufacturing was completed in a central shop and exported for profit. It was significant that several new industries came along while others faded into obsolescence. Modernization in several trades increased the fortunes while reducing the labor. The increase in wealth

Above: Another limited but necessary necessary industry in the Cape Cod towns was the village blacksmith. This shop was in Orleans and the identification on the photograph was "Fulcher's Blacksmith Shop." The mainstay of the business was horseshoes because most horses need attention to their hooves every four to six weeks. *Photo by H. K. Cummings.* Below: The cranberry industry had an early start on Cape Cod when a Dennis man accidently discovered a good way to cultivate the tart fruit. This photo is of a group of people picking cranberries on Daniel Crocker's bog in Yarmouth, circa 1890. *Photo from the collection of Matthews C. Hallet, Yarmouthport, Mass.*

Above: Another profitable industry on Cape Cod was the manufacture of pants. In Orleans, this large structure was one of the locations used to make the garments. **Below:** An interior view of the pants factory shown above. Men and women were employed and a large number of people worked in the manufacture. *Photos by H. K. Cummings.*

A group of workers posed for a picture outside one of the factories in
Orleans. There were eighty-eight persons, both male and female, in the photograph.
These people worked for the firm of Cummmings and Howes which was founded in
1873. By 1890, there were almost 200 persons employed in the manufacture of
overalls. This industry was a welcome addition to the employment conditions for Cape
Cod in the later part of the nineteenth century. In addition to the workers at the
factory, there many others doing piecework in the homes. There were several other
small industries spread over Cape Cod in that era. The Author's Grandmother is one
of the young ladies seated in the front row. *Photo by H. K. Cummings.*

The Nobscusset House and cottages in Dennis. This large hotel was one of several on Cape Cod in the later part of the nineteenth century when tourism began to flourish on Cape Cod. This large building on the right later burned down but the two cottages behind it are still there today. *Photo by H. K. Cummings.*

In the middle of the nineteenth century, the Shiverick Shipyard on Sesuit Creek in East Dennis built large ocean going clipper ships for the world trade. There are no remains of the ship-ways today but a bronze plaque at the head of the harbor remembers the events that occurred in those historic times. *Photo by William P. Quinn.*

THE SHIVERICK SHIPYARD

In Commemoration of an industrial enterprise instituted by Christopher Hall, a shipowner and retired shipmaster in cooperation with David, Asa and Paul Shiverick, shipbuilders; thereby eight sailing ships of approximately one thousand tons register each and four schooners of smaller size were built with the after ends of their keels resting about fifty feet south southeast of this spot. The names of these vessels and the dates of their construction are recorded on the margins hereof, and as a memorial to nobility of character exemplfied in acts and deeds, that showered unnumbered blessings on this community while the actors lived, yet left a more precious heritage to succeeding generations in examples of high conception of human interests, of lofty, beautiful ideals masterfully attained.

SHIPS:

Revenue 1848-50	Hippogriffe 1851-52
Belle of the West 1852-53	Kit Carson 1853-54
Wild Hunter 1854-55	Webfoot 1855-56
Christopher Hall 1857-58	Ellen Sears 1862-63

SCHOONERS:

Watson Baker 1853	J.K. Baker 1853
Searsville 1854	West Wind 1858-59

brought the desire for the refinements of life among the middle and upper classes.

The people in the town of Dennis were not only famous for pioneering saltworks and cranberries but deepwater square-rigged ships were launched from Sesuit Creek in East Dennis. Asa Shiverick began a shipyard at Sesuit harbor on Quivet Neck in Dennis during the 1820's and built his share of brigs, schooners and sloops. His sons, Asa, Jr., Paul and David, entered the business in 1848. They built large clipper ships that were known the world over. There is today a monument with a brass plaque describing the early operations here and listing the several vessels that entered the waters of this harbor. The sloop *Star,* used to carry salt manufactured at Dennis, was just one of many ships constructed on the banks of Sesuit Creek. Near the shipyard, Asa Shiverick operated many vats of saltworks.

There was a village of considerable size here at that time complete with two general stores, a steaming plant for bending ship timbers, a blacksmith shop, carpenter shop, caulker's shop, joiner shop and several other buildings for the outfitting of the vessel being constructed on the ways. The larger ships were all over one thousand tons burden and after launching went to Boston under jury rig or were towed there for the final outfitting. The *Revenue* (1849), and *Hippogriffe* (1852) were the first two large vessels built here and these were followed by the *Belle of the West* (1853), the *Kit Carson* (1854), the *Wild Hunter* (1855), the *Webfoot* (1856), the *Christopher Hall* (1858) and the *Ellen Sears,* (1863).

These ships were fine examples of the American shipbuiders skill. They were beautiful and fast vessels reflecting the pride in construction from the little yard on Cape Cod Bay. Along the Atlantic coast the Shiverick ships were not as well known as those of Donald McKay of Boston or the larger yards in Maine but they were admired and envied in all of the foreign ports they touched. The *Belle of the West* was considered to be one of the most beautiful clippers anywhere. The history of these Dennis ships and the men who sailed them is another exciting chapter in the annals of Cape Cod.

Today, the tourist industry dominates the Cape Cod economy. Some people believe that Henry David Thoreau was the first summer visitor to the Cape but he was engaged in gathering material for his writings and he may not have been in the tourist category. There is evidence, however, of some summer visitors spending the season here before the Civil War. The growing prosperity in Barnstable County was reflected by an increase in leisure time for the well-to-do. The work ethic was still strong but more and more manufactured goods were being imported from the cities. As a result of this, the Cape women spent less time at the spinning wheel or the loom. The Barnstable Patriot carried an article, in the September 1st edition in 1857, about some grand social activities that took place in Brewster during the summer of that year.

"Brewster, Cape Cod, Aug. 20, 1857 - The town of Brewster is uncommonly lively this season. A much larger number of visitors than usual are here for recreation. The schooner *Eliza J. Kelley*, Capt. Chase, who, by-the-bye, is not only a skillful navigator, but a gentleman always attentive to the wants of his passengers. He is communicative to all on board, and the number during the past two months, has been very large. Thirty-four passengers, mostly ladies were counted on one trip. The packet makes two trips per week, and is a very fast sailer.

"From the number of gaily dressed ladies, that are seen driving, walking, or bathing at Brewster, one would be led to think that it was a fashionable watering place instead of the rural and sandy town of Brewster, on Cape Cod. Often have we seen parties of twenty-five to thirty persons on their way up to the Pond, with fish rods, and the implements necessary for making a chowder, and preparing for a good time generally. On one occasion, as one of their wagons, in which was seated eight ladies, was turning up to the Mansion House, the lady who held the ribbons proposed driving up in style, which she did in a manner not very pleasant. She overturned the wagon, precipitating the eight ladies in the sand. However, no one was seriously injured, and it served to make a grand laugh for the spectators.

"One of our neighbors drives four splendid dapple greys to a large wagon with four seats, which will accommodate sixteen persons, and when filled with beautiful ladies, as it often is, it makes a sight worth seeing.

"On Tuesday evening a grand fancy ball came off at the Town Hall, and it was a splendid affair. The ladies were dressed superbly. Miss C____, as Beatrice, appeared in a striped pink and white satin under dress, trimmed with three white lace flounces bordered with crimson with a pink opera cape carelessly thrown over the shoulders. Miss E.C_____, was in the costume of a Turkish lady, and looked charmingly. Miss L.C____, represented Pocahontas. Miss O.B_____, a nun. Miss L.J.P., from Boston, in pink flounce. Miss P____, looked brilliant, and danced gracefully. This lady attracted great attention. Miss S____, wore the dress of Savotti, a fish woman, and was generally admired. Miss W____, of Boston was very gaily attired, and won the admiration of all by her dignified and graceful appearance. The dancing was kept up until a late hour, when the company dispersed, highly pleased with the fancy ball. This, we believe, was the first fancy ball given in Brewster.

"The towns on the Cape are among the most attractive on the shore for summer resorts, and as the means of communication with the city increases, they will continue to attract notice."

THE KNOWLES CONNECTION

Large families were common in the seventeenth and eighteenth centuries because many hands were needed to produce the goods for the whole family. Another reason was infant mortality. A family of ten or twelve children would have sometimes suffered the loss, at birth, of an additional two or three infants. Sometimes the mother was lost in childbirth. In those days, the mother's unmarried sister usually came to tend the house and often ended up marrying the brother-in-law to carry on the family. The eldest boy, the senior member of the next generation, usually inherited his father's property. The other male siblings went to sea or worked for the father and then the older brother. The girls were taught the fundamentals of raising a family. Sewing, spinning, weaving, cooking and sometimes tending the saltworks, were all part of a daughters everyday life.

The Knowles family began on Cape Cod in the early part of the seventeenth century and continues today in Eastham. Richard Knowles was born in England circa 1615-1620. He married Ruth Bower on August 15, 1639, in Plymouth, Massachusetts. The Knowles family vital information is told in the genealogy by Virginia Knowles Hufbauer, published in 1974. Many Cape Cod families are blessed with longevity. The Knowles line has carried on this tradition through several generations and some of the decendants have lived on the same property in Eastham for more than two hundred years. This is a sincere compliment to the quality of life on Cape Cod. It is known that, initially, Richard settled in Eastham around 1654 in the area that is now Orleans. He was a shipmaster and his lands were at the head of Town Cove. He had ten children. His eldest son was John. From these children the family has multiplied into thousands of descendants all over the United States. The purpose of this information herewith is to establish the lineage and explain the connection of two deeds containing saltworks, passed back and forth in the family. This story will follow only one line of the Knowles family down to the tenth generation.

In the second generation, John was born and lived in Eastham and there were three children in his family. John's birth date was not listed but he was married to Apphia Bangs at Eastham in 1670, and their three children were Edward in 1671, John, Jr., in 1673, and Rebecca in 1674. Unfortunately, John was killed in an Indian raid at Taunton, Massachusetts in June, 1675, leaving his three children as orphans.

The third generation, Colonel John Knowles, was born in Eastham in 1673, and died there in 1757. Orphaned at two years old, he was brought up by his uncle, Joshua Bangs. Colonel Knowles owned land in Eastham at the head of town cove. (Later, Orleans.) He was married twice. The first wife, Mary Sears, bore him eight children. The second wife was Rebecca Chanle. There were no children from this union.

Continuing to the fourth generation, Colonel Willard Knowles was born, November, 1711, and died March 1786, at Eastham. He commanded the Second Barnstable Regiment and was a Justice of the Peace. He inherited from his father the property in Eastham, just north of the old cemetery, some of which is still in the family today. He was married in 1733 to Bethia Atwood of Eastham and they had eleven children. The property was bequeathed to his two youngest sons.

William Knowles was the fifth generation in this line. He was born May, 1755, and died August, 1830, at Eastham. He married Rebecca Freeman and they had nine children. He was a farmer. The genealogy states that he was "engaged extensively in the salt business." He also had a store.

In the sixth generation, Freeman Knowles was born in 1779, and died in 1838, at Eastham. He married Martha Mayo in December, 1813. They had seven children. The genealogy relates that "He was an aggresive business man, and bought up most of the land on both sides of the Town Cove Road and below the ancient Eastham Cemetery."

The next in line was the seventh generation, another Freeman Knowles, born October, 1821, and died March, 1909, in Eastham. He married Joanna Smith in April, 1848. They had four children. He was the author of the deed in 1840, of lands to Isaiah Doane, Mariner.

For the eighth generation, James Paxton Knowles was born April,

1873, and died Sept. 1932. He married Millie Louise Walker in Eastham and they had two children.

Near the end of the line, the ninth generation member is James Paxton Knowles, Jr., who was born December 1917, in Eastham and is still living. He is the father of two children, James H. Knowles, who is the tenth generation and his sister Anne M. Knowles. The continuation of the family name in this lineage will end with the present James H. Knowles as he does not have any sons. His father, James P. Knowles Jr., lives in Eastham in a house built on land owned by James Paxton Knowles, Sr. This is one line of descendants of Richard Knowles in Eastham from the middle of the seventeenth century to the later part of the twentieth century.

Saltworks were part of the real estate and as such, could be bought and sold. Several early deeds have surfaced and two of these disclose an unusual sale and resale that occurred at Eastham. In one deed, dated November 30, 1840, Freeman Knowles of Eastham, Yeoman, (7th Gen.) sold for twenty-five hundred dollars, to Isaiah Doane, Mariner: "his heirs and assigns, All my Real Estate situated in Eastham, Orleans and Wellfleet, consisting of cleared lands, Woodlands, Meadow, Swamp, buildings and Salt Works - for the boundaries and description reference may be had to my deeds of the same. Also all my personal Estate, consisting of Horses, Cattle, Sheep, Hog, Beds, Bedding, Household furniture, Salt Scow boat &c &c with all the privileges and appurtenances to the above belongings."

The deed was signed by Freeman Knowles in the presence of Lothrop Davis, Justice of the Peace.

It would appear that Freeman Knowles (7th Gen.) had sold all of his land together with the saltworks and farm with animals etc. This is the land he had inherited (or purchased) from his father, the sixth generation Freeman Knowles of Eastham.

On September 12, 1842, Isaiah Doane of Eastham, Mariner, sold for the price of twenty-five hundred dollars, to Freeman Knowles, Yeoman:

"his heirs and assigns, All the Real Estate, consisting of Cleared lands, Woodland, Meadow, Swamp, buildings and Salt Works situated in

This is a reproduction of a deed dated November 30, 1840 from **Freeman Knowles** of Eastham, to **Isaiah Doane**. All lands, buildings, personal estate and saltworks were sold for $2,500.

Eastham, Orleans and Wellfleet, which was conveyed to me by said Freeman Knowles by deed bearing date November 30, A.D. 1840. Also all the personal estate conveyed to me by said deed, consisting of Horses, Cattle, Sheep, Hog, Beds Bedding, Household furniture, Salt Scow boat &c &c."

This deed contained a key witness:

"I the said Isaiah Doane, with Temperance, my wife, who acquits her right to dower, in the above named property."

The deed was signed by Isaiah Doane in the presence of Lothrop Davis, Justice of the Peace.

This property contained saltworks and was sold in 1840. It was bought back in 1842 for the same price. There is a mystery surrounding this transfer of property. The deeds give no explanations as to why the property was conveyed in this manner. However, a search through the Knowles and Doane genealogies may have provided a partial solution to the puzzle.

Quoting from the Knowles Genealogy: "Freeman Knowles, (6th Gen.) Son of William and Rebecca (Freeman) Knowles was born on November 27, 1779 at Eastham and died there June 22, 1838. He married Martha Mayo of Eastham and they had seven children. He was an aggressive business man, and bought up most of the land on both sides of the Town Cove Road and below the ancient Eastham Cemetery. He is said to have built a flat-roofed house which stands a little north from the cemetery and is still in the possession of his descendants."

This house still stands beside Route 6 in Eastham but with a hip roof. Some of the the lands conveyed were, no doubt, the ones mentioned in the above deeds. The answer lies in the fact that Temperance Doane was the eldest child of Freeman Knowles, (6th Gen.) the senior of that name, and she was married to Isaiah Doane. She was the sister of Freeman Knowles, (7th Gen.) the junior of that name. Isaiah Doane died in 1846. It can probably be assumed that Doane, a mariner, had quit the sea and decided to settle down and make his living ashore; Freeman Knowles, (Sr.) had died in 1838 and his property apparently went to the next eligible son in

This is a reproduction of the deed from Isaiah Doane to Freeman Knowles. It was dated September 6, 1842. The property was sold back to Mr. Knowles for the same price it was purchased for two years earlier.

line or may have been divided between the children. Freeman (Jr.) sold his property with the saltworks to Isaiah Doane. Two years later, Doane may have been taken sick with a debilitating illness and it is possible that he was physically unable to carry on the business. He may have had to sell the property back to his brother-in-law so as to provide his wife with money for living expenses. Much of this is of course supposition but given the conditions and lifestyles in that era, it might be the reason for the property transfers but there may be other unknown factors involved. Because he died in 1846, it was probably sickness that caused him to sell the property back to his brother-in-law.

There were other property deeds in the group studied and the decline of the saltworks industry during that era showed the prices gradually decreasing as time passed. In 1862, after the industry had been failing for twenty years, eighteen hundred feet of works sold for only one hundred and ten dollars.

The saltworks described in the Knowles - Doane deeds were located in Eastham on the Town cove (arrow) and were part of a large tract of land owned by the Knowles family in the 1840's.

The 1851 map of the central part of the town of Sandwich shows where the Sandwich Glass Works were situated. The population around the area was very dense. Nearly the same roads exist today in the town except the large industrial area has disappeared.

The Upper Cape Towns

Chapter Six

Barnstable County comprises the entire peninsula of Cape Cod. The fifteen towns of today began in the 1600's as four separate townships; Sandwich, Barnstable, Yarmouth and Nauset. The first town settled on the Cape was Sandwich in 1637. Barnstable and Yarmouth were next in 1639. The fourth, settled in 1644, was Nauset. Later, in 1651 the name was changed to Eastham. The town of Falmouth was settled in 1661 and incorporated in 1686. The Indian lands of Mashpee were set off in 1682 and they were incorporated as the plantation of Marshpee on June 14, 1763.

As the years passed, those settlements east of Barnstable divided into smaller towns. In 1794, Yarmouth split up and Dennis became a separate town. In 1694, Harwich was separated from Eastham; the Indians called it Satucket. Brewster later split from Harwich in 1803. Eastham was divided into five towns. Truro separated in 1705 as the town of Dangerfield but that was changed to Truro in 1709. Provincetown separated from Truro in 1727. Chatham was first called Monomoyick but it was incorporated with its present name in 1712. Wellfleet became a town in 1763 and finally Orleans separated from Eastham in 1797. The last town to be incorporated was Bourne which separated from Sandwich in 1884.

The first town on Cape Cod was Sandwich, situated on the northwest corner of the county. Most of the saltworks there were located on Buzzards Bay in what is now the town of Bourne. The number of salt evaporators was small compared to the rest of the Cape. The

The 1849 map locates the saltworks around the town of Falmouth. There were several hundred feet of evaporators along the shores of the town. The area on the left hand side of the map is where the town center is today.

Commonwealth of Massachusetts had a tax list for the year 1831 and the figures for Sandwich showed 162,666 superficial feet of saltworks. Ten years later the number had been reduced to 93,000. Because of the decline in the industry, the figure in 1850 was down to 2,000 feet.

There were several packet vessels from the town of Sandwich. Captain Roland Gibbs had the sloop *Polly* and Captain Sewall Fessenden had the sloop *Splendid*, both running from Sandwich to Boston in the 1820's. Later Captain Charles Nye ran the sloop *Charles*, which was built in Sandwich. Deming Jarves of the Sandwich Glass Factory built the sloop *Sandwich* to carry passengers and glass. Later, when he had a dispute with the railroad over freight rates, Mr. Jarves built the steamer *Acorn* to carry his glass to Boston. A couple of others were the *Nancy Finley* and the *Wm. G. Eddie*.

The town of Falmouth is at the southwest corner of Cape Cod with many harbors and inlets. It was a natural area for the manufacture of salt. The Massachusetts tax list for 1831 showed 1,830,860 superficial feet of works. In 1841 the number was down slightly to 1,659,020 and in 1850 it was 874,200. There were several saltworks owners listed in Deyo's History:

"In this, the long belt of sea shore and the salt ponds within its borders gave the town superior advantages. Logs were laid out into clearer and salter water, which was pumped by salt-mills into vats and reservoirs on high ground, and there evaporated. The land between salt and fresh ponds was covered with sheds with revolving roofs to the evaporating vats. At that early day the business was lucrative, salt bringing one dollar per bushel at the works. Ephraim Sanford, one of the later manufacturers, was wont to make trips to New York during the war of 1812, and could clear one hundred dollars on each trip. He had red sails to avoid notice at night. As among other enterprises of the day, those engaged in salt-making were captains John Crocker, Weston Jenkins, Elijah Swift and Silas Jones (father of the present [1890] bank president), who were succeeded by Ephraim Sanford, Captain John Butler, Knowles Butler and Davis and John Hatch; and among the late owners were Silas and Thomas Lawrence, John

An 1849 map around Quamquisset harbor (now Quisset) near Woods Hole in Falmouth locates some large acreage of saltworks.

Dimmock, Nymphus Davis and Silas Davis. Edmund Davis was the last to carry on the business, and he continued until he found it more advantageous to sell out his site on the 'Heights' for cottage lots. The business declined before the middle of the century, but was carried on to a limited extent as late as 1865."

"Woods Hole: Owners listed are Ward M. Parker, John Parker, Ephraim Eldridge and Jabez Davis."

"West Falmouth: Nearly all the families were Quakers. Agriculture was the first industrial resource, but it was at one time almost entirely superseded by salt-making, which became important and profitable. Nearly all the people were interested in its manufacture. Daniel Bowerman, William and Theophilus Gifford, Ephraim Sanford, Marcus and George W. Wicks, Adrian Davis, Joseph and Stephen Dillingham, Elijah, Seth, Daniel, Joseph, Silas and Moses Swift, James and Silas Gifford, Benjamin Crowell, Walter Davis and Zebulon Bowman, in their time, were conspicuous in the manufacture of salt. The last works were operated by Nathaniel Eldred, a retired sea captain, who sold his plant to S.F. Swift, who discontinued in 1871."

The packet vessels that ran from Falmouth did not go to Boston but to New Bedford. The Cape Cod Canal did not exist in those early times. The sloops *Henry Clay, Swift* and *Temperance* were in service for a number of years. From West Falmouth, the sloops *Nile* and *Peerless*. These ran to New Bedford on a regular basis until the railroad put them out of business.

The present town of Mashpee had no saltworks enrolled on the tax list for any of the reported years. For a long time, the name was spelled "Marshpee". The Indian area had the smallest shoreline of any of the Cape towns and therefore it may be that no works were built along the waterfront in that town. None was drawn in on the early topographical maps.

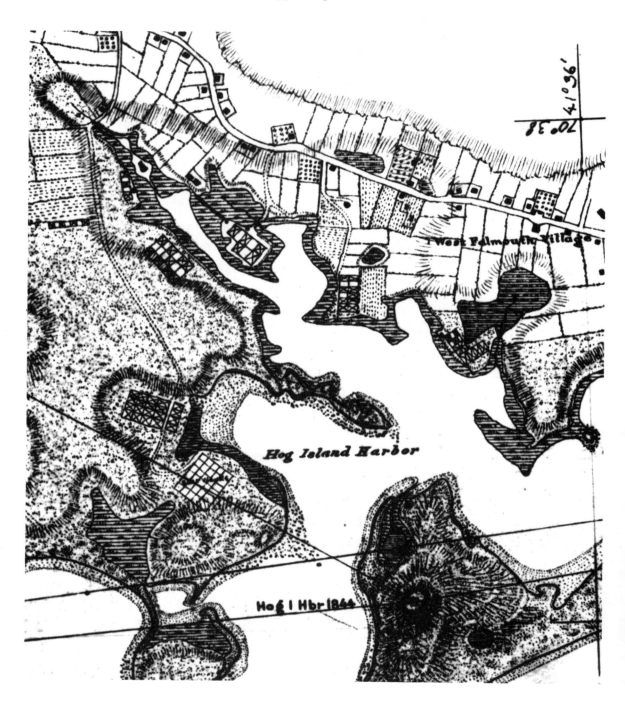

Another area in West Falmouth shows a large area of saltworks. The squares with x's in them depict the salt vats around Hog Island Harbor.

Above:The salt mills at the Crocker saltworks in Barnstable. The size of the pumps can be determined in relation to the man standing beside the wind vanes. A six-foot man would indicate that the diameter of the mill vanes is about eighteen feet with about twenty feet of vane area to catch the wind. The wooden pipes leading to the salt vats were hollowed out logs. They were either drilled or burned out. The pipes were then connected together and sealed with white lead. **Below:** The saltworks of Loring Crocker in Barnstable covered a vast area of the land next to the present day Barnstable Harbor. In this photo there are two horses and buggies. One of these may be a working rig for the man tending the saltworks. *Photos from the collection of Louis Cataldo, Barnstable, Mass.*

A long view of the Loring Crocker saltworks in Barnstable. This view was probably taken from across the creek shown in the map on page 115. *Photo from the collection of Louis Cataldo, Barnstable, Mass.*

The largest town on the Cape is Barnstable, located in the central part of the peninsula and running from Cape Cod Bay to Nantucket Sound. It is the shire town of Barnstable County. Loring Crocker had his saltworks on the common fields at Barnstable Village. The tax lists showed that in 1831 there were 920,750 superficial feet of saltworks here. In 1841 the number came down slightly to 876,450. In 1850 the saltworks had begun their decline and the number was 94,000. The owners were listed in Deyo's History:

"Nathaniel Gorham boiled sea water and made salt, on Sandy Neck, during the revolutionary war. Many of the present residents of Barnstable village remember when the "Common Field" - the marsh in the rear of the Unitarian church - was a field of salt works. Loring Crocker, grandfather of Alfred Crocker, was the pioneer in this industry on the common field. In 1804 he bought of Isaac Bacon several acres of land with the right to the salt water and the privilege of placing pumps. He afterward, in 1832, bought sixteen hundred running feet of Samuel Whitman, who had succeeded Lothrup Tucker; then east of this he purchased in 1836, works of Mrs. Sturgis; and he bought Asa Young's works, so that when Loring Crocker died, in the fall of 1843, he was the owner of seventeen thousand running feet of vats, most of which were on the Common field.

"After Loring Crocker died, his sons, Nathan and Loring operated the works up to 1856. Loring bought out his brother and operated them until 1872. Loring was the father of Alfred Crocker of Barnstable who worked on the family saltworks.

"Other owners: Nathaniel Gorham; Amos Otis; William Dixon; Henry L. Hopkins who sold to Alvin Howes who sold to Truman D. Eldredge.

"Osterville: owners were: Thomas Ames; Seth Goodspeed, Ebenezer Scudder, George Hinckley; Jacob Lovell had works near O.D. Lovell's boat house, first from the eastward; he used two wind mills to pump the water to the works. Henry Lovell's was next west, then came Deacon Scudder's then George Lovell's.

"Hyannis: During the war of 1812 salt was a prominent industry. Alvin Snow, Henry and Joshua Hallett had extensive works where is now the Sears lumber yard; A.W. Lovell manufactured near the present lumber yard of B.F. Crocker & Co. This like most of the works, was discontinued about 1831. Lot Crocker had works where his descendants now reside, and Ebenezer Bacon's were adjoining. Zenas Gage engaged in the manufacture near his wharf; Simeon Freeman had works at Dunbar Point, and Zenas D. Bassett and Warren Hallett had their works next west. Other manufacturers were Elnathan Lewis, Warren and David Hinckley, and Gorham Lovell.

"Hyannisport: Frederick Scudder, David Hinckley, Deacon James Marchant and Freeman Marchant made salt here soon after 1800."

There were several Barnstable packets. In the early 1800's, the schooner *Comet,* was running from Barnstable to Boston. The sloop *Independence,* also ran here and was burned by the British during the War of 1812. There were four well known packets that ran after the war, the schooners *Globe, Volant, Sappho* and *Flavilla,* were all built in Barnstable as was the sloop *Freedom.* Other sloops engaged in service were the *Science, James Lawrence, Velocity* and *Mail.* A couple of steamboats were running from Barnstable in the 1840's. The *Express* and the *Yacht* made regular trips to Boston. The sailing packets did not fade away entirely when the steamboats began running. An advertisement on the front page of the Yarmouth Register on June 8, 1848 was designed for business:

"NOTICE: The new and elegant schr. Pizarro has been bought expressly for a Packet to run the ensuing season between Hyannis and New York, touching at intermediate places if required. All orders attended to with punctuality and despatch. Smallest favors thankfully received. For freight or passage apply to Eli Hinckley, Hyannis Port, Baxter & Bragg, at their wharf, Hyannis, or to the master on board.

Heman B. Chase, Master., Hyannis, May 18, 1848."

Above: This aerial photograph taken in modern times shows the area where the Crocker saltworks were located near Barnstable Harbor. The area is full of summer cottages today. **Below:** The 1849 map of Barnstable shows the large area of saltworks belonging to Loring Crocker. The exact spot where he mounted his cannon in 1814 to protect his works is not marked but they were probably near the shoreline.

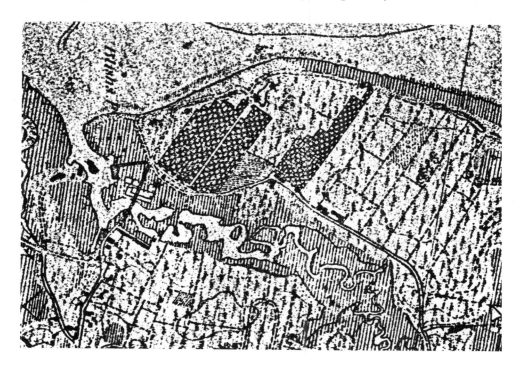

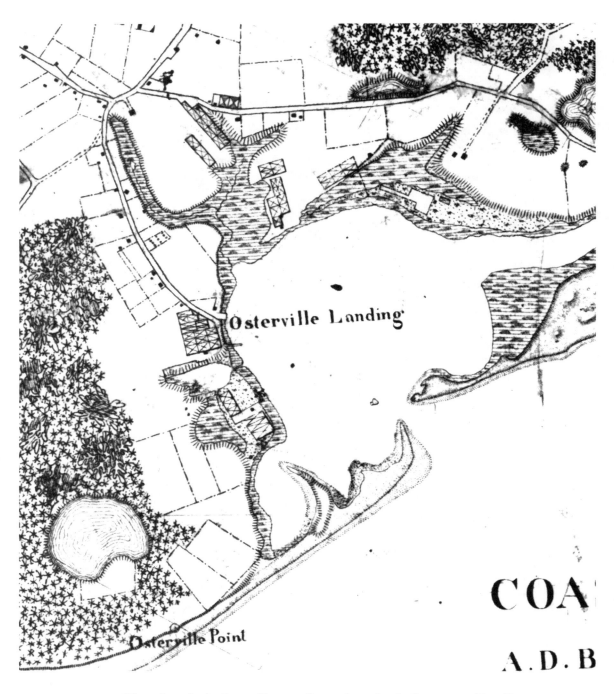

The saltworks in Osterville were located at what is the present East Bay near Wianno. There were several hundred feet of evaporators as depicted in the 1849 U.S. Coast Survey map.

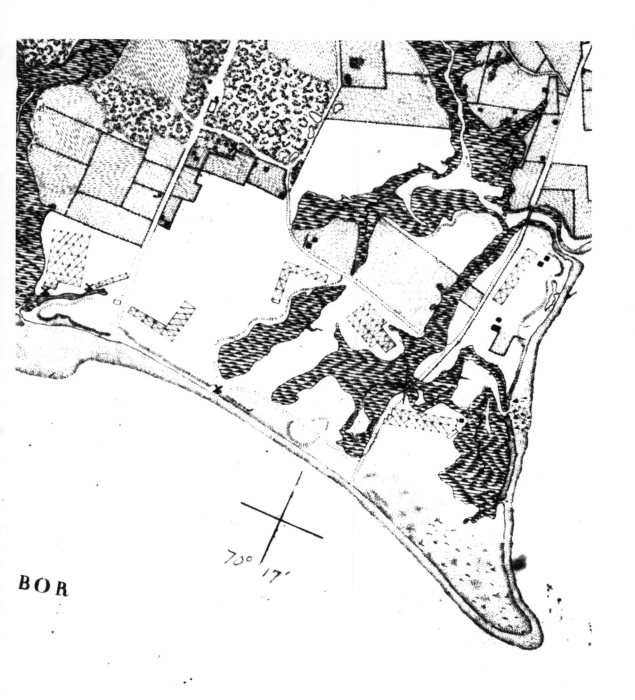

BOR

The Hyannis saltworks were located near Dunbar Point on Lewis Bay and Hyannis harbor. The small x near the center of the map on the beach is the site of a salt mill.

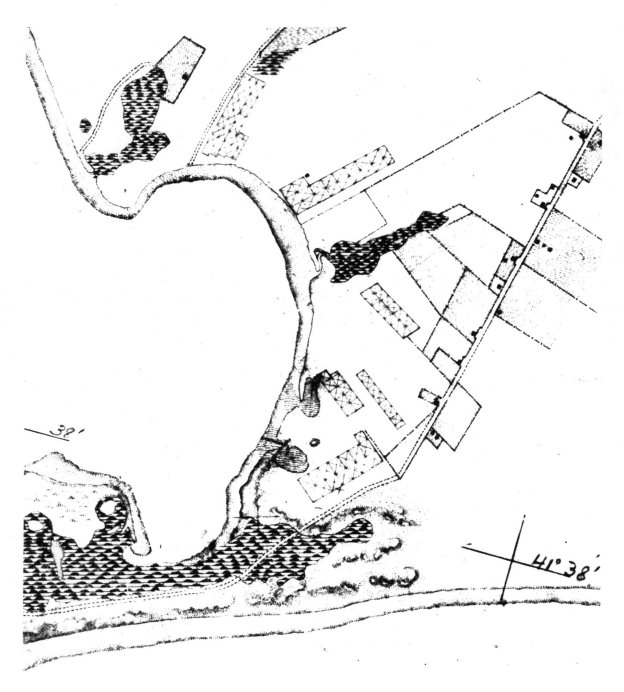

In West Yarmouth on Lewis Bay there were several saltworks near today's Seagull Beach as shown in the 1849 Coast Survey map. The road on the bottom part of the map leads to Great Island.

The Mid Cape Towns

The first town east of Barnstable is Yarmouth. It was originally called Mattacheese by the Indians. On the south shore was a large salt evaporating industry. There was also a magnesia factory located on Bass River near the saltworks. In 1831, the Massachusetts tax list showed the town had 764,280 superficial feet of saltworks. In 1841 that number had grown to 2,289,910 feet. In 1850 the amount was reduced to 1,577,300, at that time it was the largest spread of saltworks on Cape Cod. The industry lasted longer here than any other town. The owners were listed in Deyo's History:

"South Yarmouth: The first salt works built here were located between the county road and Bass River, nearly opposite the present site of Standish Hall, upon land sold by John Kelley to Isaiah Crowell, Seth Kelley and Zeno Kelley, for that purpose in 1811. Subsequently, Abiel Akin, Russell Davis, Stephen Smith, Robert Wing, David K. Akin, George Wing, Daniel Wing, Lewis Crowell and Abraham Sherman conducted the industry quite extensively and with good degree of success. These works have been kept repaired and in use until the past few years; the long rows of covered vats, still visible in the west part of the village are still venerable in their

The saltworks at Yarmouth on Bass River in the late 1800's. These works were still in operation at the time. There is water in the vats and sails on the saltmill in the background. The man tending the works is near the center of the picture while three children appear to be walking through the area. *Photo by H.K. Cummings.*

decay. Robert Wing was an extensive manufacturer, whose works are now extant at Lower Village, and owned by David Kelley. David Smith built his on Bass river above the bridge, and Edward Gifford's were still to the north. Prince Gifford erected works northwest of the present main street, on land now belonging to his heirs. In fact this part of the town contained more feet of works than any other; and the residences of Stephen Wing and others along the southerly side of the street are built where stood these vast plants. The more recent manufacturers were Hatsel Crosby, Isaiah Crocker, Asa Covil, Barnabas Sears, Loren Baker, Francis Wood and Howes Berry. The manufacture of magnesia has also been discontinued for two years, (1890) Wing Brothers being the last engaged in it. F. Fearing established the trade here, in 1855. The decline in salt manufacture marked the bounds of the magnesia business here."

Captain Levi Crowell of Yarmouth kept a diary of his life and there is an interesting entry about saltworks:

"Major Obed Baxter and his son, Obed, Jr., each had a line of saltworks and a mill on the south shore of Bass River, adjoining my father's landing and wharf on the east. Each of them had a large salt store. They made and sold to the fishermen quite a quantity of salt. I helped in getting out the salt from the tanks and rolling it in a wheelbarrow to the salt store of Major Obed Baxter when I was nineteen years old, and I was paid fifty cents for my day's work. At that time, there were a great many saltworks in South Yarmouth, on the west bank of Bass River beginning a short distance below Bass River bridge and extending down to the store of Braddock Matthews. The entire river bank was one line of saltworks and salt mills, and a large quantity of salt was made and shipped to New York for sale.

"My grandfather, Thomas Crowell, was born January 18, 1760 and died September 5, 1855, aged ninety-five. His house was about 100 yards northeast of my house with a barn just west of my big garden. He had a small windmill and a number of saltworks on the north shore of the little cove, and he made quite a quantity of salt. These saltworks were taken up [dismantled] about 1853. The house and barn fell into disrepair in the latter years of my grandfather's long life and were torn down after he died in 1855."

SALT-WORKS.—South Yarmouth.   Built during the War of 1812.

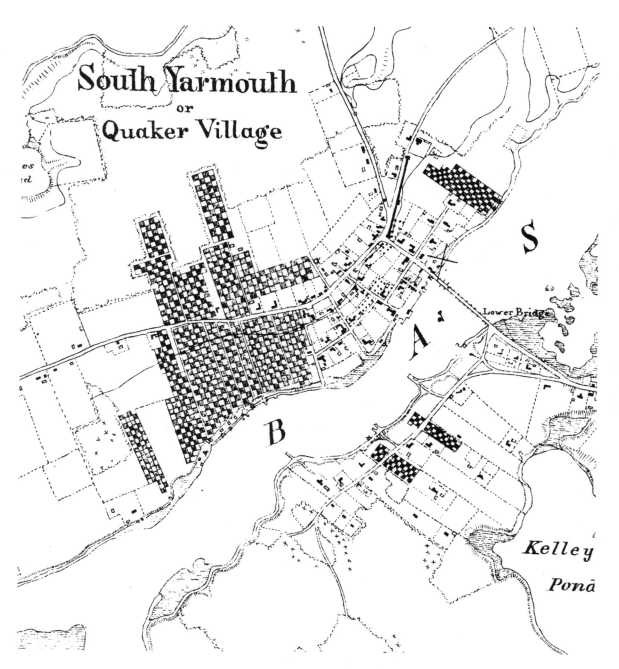

The 1850 Coast Survey map of Yarmouth located a vast area of saltworks on the Bass River. There were several more upstream and on the opposite shores in West Dennis. This was one of the largest concentrations of evaporators on Cape Cod.

Above: A modern aerial photograph of Bass River in Yarmouth taken at same location where the saltworks were located on the river. Today the entire acreage is filled with houses. The waterfront is now a summer playground for yachtsmen. *Aerial Photo by William P. Quinn.*

Above: The picture is titled "Old Saltworks, S. Yarmouth, Mass. The Judah Baker windmill is on the right side of the photo. It is still in nearly the same area today. **Below:** This photo is taken from an old post card and it is another area of the saltworks at Bass River with the salt mills near the water. Drying rooms and salt vats surround the land next to the dwelling houses in the background. *Photos courtesy of Alec & Audrey Todd, Yarmouth, Mass.*

Four salt mills in a row in this photo titled "Saltworks at East Yarmouth." The title locates them near the large area of works on Bass River. *Photo from the Author's collection.*

Some of the early packets along the Yarmouth bay shore were the sloops *Martha Jane, Emerald, Flight,* and *Commodore Hull.* Later the schooner *Yarmouth* was carrying freight and passengers to Boston. Some later packets listed were the *Herit Meriah, Yarmouth* and the schooner *H.S. Barnes.* The last coaster in Bass River was the *David K. Akin,* used to carry coal from New Jersey to Yarmouth.

Above: Bass River in Yarmouth was a busy waterway in the nineteenth century as can be seen in this photograph taken on the Dennis side of the river. On the opposite bank the coal schooner *David K. Akin* was moored with a headsail raised. In the immediate foreground a dismasted and abandoned hull served as a pier for catboats, which were the sport craft of that time. Another coastal schooner was tied up in front of a waterfront store. *Photo courtesy of Alec & Audrey Todd, Yarmouth, Mass.* **Below:** What appears to be the schooner *Hattie* was sunk near James Crowell's store. The sign on the side of the store read: James Crowell - Coal, Corn, Flour, Oats, Feed &c. *Photo from the Author's collection.*

   Above: This photograph appears to have been taken from the same location as the top photo on page 126 but at a later date. The old hulk was still there but it had deteriorated. There were some anchor draggers tied up alongside and the same schooner was tied up in front of Crowell's store. On the opposite bank the *David K. Akin* was moored alongside her Yarmouth pier. **Below:** The Bass River bridge taken from the Dennis side of the river with two anchor draggers moored near the bridge. *Photos courtesy Alec & Audrey Todd, Yarmouth, Mass.*

BASS RIVER AND VILLAGE OF SOUTH YARMOUTH IN 1874
The year BASS RIVER SAVINGS BANK *was Founded*

The Bass River Savings Bank was founded in 1874 and in 1974 they commissioned a tile to depict the town as it was a century before. The tile shows what appears to be the schooner *David K. Akin* on the other side of the river, the Bass River toll bridge and in the foreground on the right are the saltworks on the Dennis side of the water.

When the salt works were torn down the lumber was used to build sheds, barns and even some houses. This photograph was taken in the cellar of a barn on Route 6A in Yarmouthport. The sub-floor is saltworks boards, over one hundred years old and are still weeping salt from the vats. The boards were sixteen to twenty inches wide and it was possible to scrape salt off them with a pen knife. *Photo by William P. Quinn.*

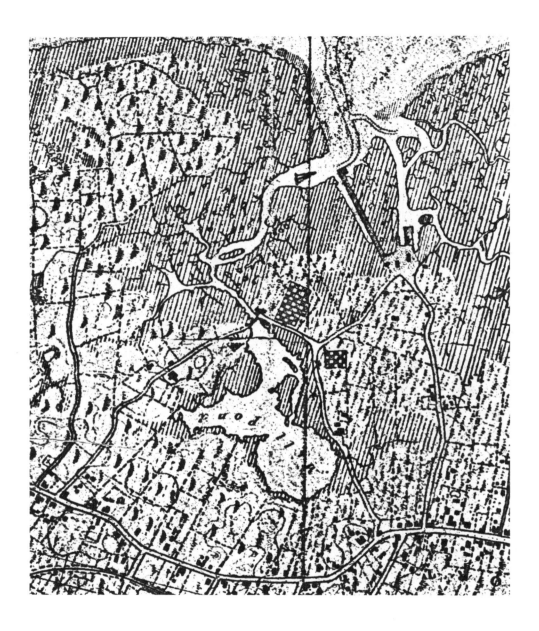

A section of the 1849 coastal survey map showing Yarmouthport, near the Mill Pond area on Cape Cod Bay. There are two large saltworks situated near the salt pond.

Above: Another view of the saltworks in Yarmouthport. These may be the ones located on the map on the previous page. *Photo courtesy of Matthews C. Hallet, Yarmouthport, Mass.* Below: A reproduction of a post card showing Main Street in Yarmouthport in 1856. The card depicts the arrival of the stagecoach in town in front of the Barnstable Bank.

Above An aerial view of Quivet Neck in East Dennis as it appears today. The saltworks are all gone and have been replaced by houses. The salt industry realized high profits in its time but the real estate is far more valuable today for beach front summer cottages. **Below:** At the east end of Quivet Neck the land is undeveloped. It is at present privately owned and owners hope to keep it that way. This area was used extensively in the manufacture of salt in the early 1800's. *Aerial photographs by William P. Quinn.*

The saltworks at East Dennis which appear to be abandoned and ready to be torn apart. The many stakes in the foreground probably supported other vats for evaporation. *Photo by H. K. Cummings.*

Going east from Yarmouth the next town is Dennis. This was the birthplace of Cape Cod saltworks. The Indian name for this place was Nobscusset. The 1831 Massachusetts tax list shows that there were 1,916,908 superficial feet of saltworks here. In 1841 the number was up to 2,439,190 and in 1850 it was reduced to 156,744. Many owners were listed in Deyo's History but as has been stated, the description of Quivet Neck was probably emblished slightly to stress the importance of the industry's origin:

"John Sears began the manufacture of salt in 1776. The entire surface of Quivet neck adjoining the bay, and the greater part of Sesuit, were covered with vats. Of the Sears and Crowell families, the first on the neck, nearly all the heads engaged in this work. Edmund Sears started his works in 1795 and his son, Edmund in 1818. In 1803 John Sears, William Crowell, John Crowell and the elder Edmund Sears started an improved set of evaporators and covers on the eastern part of Quivet neck; and one day when they were discussing a proper name for the works, William Crowell suggested the name "John Sears Folly," which was adopted. In 1804 Jacob Sears built works. Daniel Sears in 1821, and Nathan F. Sears in 1823. Others who were interested were Joshua, Ezra, Thomas and Elkanah Sears, sr. and jr.; also Joseph, Edward and Major John Sears of Brewster, had works on Quivet neck. Ten thousand feet in East Dennis were owned by Kenelm, Isaac, Abraham and Nathaniel Winslow, and Isaac, Abraham and John Chapman owned and ran other works here. Still later and further west we find Lothrop Howes, Judah Paddock and his son and Enoch and Daniel Hall engaged in the manufacture of salt. On Sesuit neck David, William and Eli Howes, Nathan Crowell, and later Asa Shiverick had works.

"It is easy to conjecture the dotted appearance of three miles of shore when the reader has read the list of enterprising men who successfully operated these plants, which, with their owners, have passed away. One, built by John Sears in 1821, and purchased of B.H. Sears in 1857, is yet to be seen, just east of Quivet harbor. William Sears, an intelligent old gentleman of eighty years, purchased them and during the summer of 1889 made salt. Barnabas H. Sears also has another works on the extreme east end of the neck. Formerly this industry was a profitable one, for the salt was easily transported by vessels to Boston markets.

"South Dennis near the Bass River Bridge; salt works were numerous here and John and Barney Baker were the principal owners."

There were several Dennis and East Dennis Packets. Perhaps the earliest service from here began in the eighteenth century. During the 19th century, the sloops *Sally,* and *Heroine* were in service, followed by the schooner *North.* In East Dennis the vessels were named *Betsey,* the schooner *Sally and Betsey,* The schooner *Eliza and Betsey,* another sloop called the *Combine,* the schooners *David Porter* and *Combine.* Most of these vessels were used in the salt freighting from East Dennis.

Tuesday, Sept. 7, 1802, The Mercury and New England Palladium
Boston, Massachusetts   No. 20, of Volume XX.

SALT MANUFACTURE

The salt manufacture was commenced at Dennis, in the County of Barnstable, in the time of the American War, when salt was two dollars a bushel. It made but slow progress, owing to the people in general having no faith in the business, and its not arriving to that state of perfection it has since, in the goodness of the salt or the cheapness of erecting the vats. Not long after they made marine salt it was discovered, that, in the winter season, by frost, Glauber salts might be made to advantage. After peace was established, (in 1783,) salt was as low as a quarter of a dollar per bushel. The manufacture was then only carried on in a small vicinity of Dennis, and it was expected by people it would subside, on account of the lowness of the price. Those that were concerned in the business were very cautious how they gave any information respecting it, but discouraged every person that had any thoughts of entering into the business, wishing to engross the manufacture to themselves; but at the very low price salt then was, people observed they continued building vats, etc. After the constitution of the United States was established, and the Government laid duties on salt, it gave such a spring to the business in the vicinity of Dennis, that it opened the eyes of the people in the neighbouring towns, and they went into the business with spirit. They found, on experience, that it netted twenty-five pr. cent, for their money, when salt commanded three quarters of a dollar pr. bushel, and Glauber salts six dollars and a half pr. hundred. There has been I imagine, more than double the number of salt vats erected in the last two years, than there was built before.

The representation that there is a sufficient quantity of salt made at the Cape for the fisheries, is erroneous, as I judge, there are consumed annually on the Cape for the cod fishery, not less than one hundred thousand bushels. The saltworks are now erected both on the north and south side of the Cape from Sandwich to Provincetown, so that it cannot be easily ascertained what quantity of salt is made annually, but I believe at least twenty thousand bushels of marine salt and fifty tons of Glauber salts. The salt is of the first quality, as respects it pureness, whiteness, and weight. It is about the size of Isle of May salt and weighs eighty weight per bushel. The Glauber salts may be made equal to any in the world, and in quantities sufficient to supply the union and the West Indies.

There is no doubt that the water which is called the bitterns, which remains after marine salt is made, is of the quality of epsom salts, and that good epsom salts might be made, and good magnesia alba from said epsom salts. The experiment has been tried, but failed on account of its not being prosecuted for want of a knowledge of the process of manufacture. The above mentioned prices will net to the manufacturer twenty-five pr. cent, after his works have got under way, which is not until the second year; and it may be an object for those monied men who wish to foster the infant manufactures of our county to put their money into this business, so long as it will net six pr. ct. clear of risk.

There is not only the advantage of saving a dollar in the country by every dollars worth of salt made, but it gives employ to an amazing number of carpenters and other workmen; lumber and nails, which are the chief articles used, are procured among ourselves. The manner of erecting the works is not easily described. Great improvements have been made.

At first it was thought necessary to make the floors with two inch plank, it is found that inch boards are sufficient. The labour cost at the beginning more than double what it does at present, owing to the labourers not being acquainted with the present mode of erecting. There are two forms for the covering and uncovering the vats at present for which the inventors have received a patent. There are very different opinions prevailing as to the two modes; in one it is carried off with shives or rollers, in the other by an iron pivot fixed in a post, which is the last invention, and diminishes the labour part in tending, one half, at least. There are doubts as to the durability of the last invention by many, but time only can determine which mode is most durable. There is no great difference in the expense.

One thousand superficial feet of works cost at present from one hundred and ten dollars to one hundred and twenty, which will net from thirty to forty bushel of salt annually after the first year (as the seasons are for goodness) and about two hundred and fifty weight Glauber salts - the present season, has been the most unfavourable, ever since salt works have been erected at the Cape, and will turn out unfavourable to the manufacturers.

If duties would be kept on they will continue to be productive to the owners, as they may calculate on twelve or fifteen pr. cent for years to come, especially if there are some measures taken to regulate the manufacture of purgative salts, otherwise they will soon be put up in such order that they will be apt to dissolve, or the credit and sale of them be ruined. The whole business is one of the happiest discoveries for the county of Barnstable that could have taken place. It being bounded for more than fifty miles on each side, with sea, and suitable places for erecting and works and the soil in many places so light as not to be fit for agriculture and in case of war, and the fisheries should in any measure fail, the making of salt would afford employment. It was carried on in the last war by boiling but the labour is much more, and the wood of so much value that it never would have answered if the present mode had not been discovered, and the boiled salt is of a much inferior quality to the salt made by the rays of the sun.

From one concerned in the manufacture.
Cape Cod, August 28, 1802

A utility building in East Dennis built from saltworks boards. The structure is used for storage and the interior view on the next page shows the salty wood. *Photo by William P. Quinn.*

A DAY AT THE SALT WORKS.

With the industry vanished from the shores of Cape Cod over a century ago, it is difficult to visualize the type of work that went on during a normal day around the evaporators. Suffice to say that the early risers of that time accomplished most of their daily chores around the home before leaving for the saltworks. Extensive research into the saltworks enables us to theorize the probable operations around an average salt evaporating plant of that era.

The first job at the work site was probably to uncover the vats, if the weather was agreeable. This job might take an hour or more depending on the number of vats under the care of the worker. A good hot sun was the ideal condition for the evaporation of sea water but even on cloudy days, some evaporation could take place but the operator had to keep his eye on the weather and cover the vats at the first sign of any rain.

An interior view of the utility building shown on the previous page shows saltworks boards, white with salt and rusty nail holes. The entire building was erected with this spare lumber. *Photo by William P. Quinn.*

Other types of work were performed during the daily operations. When the vat was ready to be emptied and evaporation had been completed to the degree where the salt was still somewhat fluid, the heavy solution had to be shoveled out of the vat and taken to the drying room. It was then spread out to dry. The transfer was accomplished with a salt-boat. A small hollowed out log designed to carry the solution and skid along the ground easily. One man could do this but because of the weight, several trips to the drying room were necessary to completely empty the vat.

If horse power were used, it was possible to empty the vat into many smaller containers in a wagon and take it to the drying room that way. The solution had to be carefully spread out for drying and this could take some of the time allotted in a man's work day. When the vat was cleaned out, the worker had only to open a valve to pass the next batch of solution down from the upper vats and fill the top vat with the salt water from the ocean pumps. The process did not end until the fall months when the sun was low in the sky and evaporation was slowed down because of cooler weather.

After the drying had been completed, the salt had to be packaged in containers for shipment to the market or to the docks for the fishing vessels. Salt was sold by the bushel to fishermen and by hogsheads when shipped off on a coastal trader or packet.

There were other chores for a worker in the salt industry. Regular maintenance was carried on during the early part of the nineteenth century when the business was expanding rapidly. The maintenance consisted of checking the roof covers for leaks and various repairs to the vats and salt mills. The transfer of water from the mills to the vats via hollowed out wooden logs probably required constant attention. There were repairs to be carried out usually after a bad storm damaged the works. The work was not considered hard labor because a bushel of salt only weighed about sixty- five pounds. The hogsheads were handled by harnessed horse power. There are no records as to what a man was paid for his labors but it was probably in keeping with other jobs in that period.

At the end of the day, the covers all had to be rolled back into place to protect the vats from night moisture. This was probably done just before the sun went down. If the vats had been covered sometime during the day because of a threat of rain, the worker could have an early supper on that day.

The Outer Cape Towns

Harwich, just east of Dennis, was another town on Cape Cod that did not have an appreciable number of saltworks. The 1831 Massachusetts tax list showed only 10,900 superficial feet in the town. In 1841 the amount was up to 106,000 feet but in 1850 there was but 2,800 feet left. Interestingly enough, there were works on Round Cove in Pleasant Bay and the rest were located on Nantucket Sound. The small amount of this industry in Harwich was probably the cause for Simeon Deyo to omit the owners in his history.

Brewster, which was also situated next to Dennis had extensive saltworks along the Bay shore. The Massachusetts tax list showed for 1831, 1,064,580 feet. In 1841 the number was down to 943,073 and in 1850 was down further to 58,670. There were contributions by Brewster men to the development of the industry. Deyo's History outlines these:

"It was estimated that in 1809 there were between sixty and seventy thousand feet of works within the township. The first to suggest the use of the pump mill in filling the vats with salt water was Major Nathaniel Freeman, of this place, in 1785. The use of the rolling roof to cover the vats in case of rain, was the invention of Reuben Sears of this place, a carpenter, in 1793."

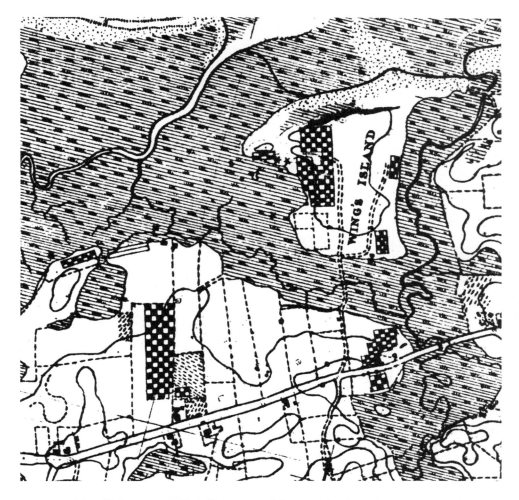

The 1849 map of West Brewster with several saltworks located. A large set of vats was situated on Wing's Island. This map overlaps the Quivet Neck map. The road in the center is the present Route 6A.

In Brewster there was a landing place for the packets at Point-of-Rocks, which was a breakwater laid out into the bay. First came the *Republic,* with Captain James Crosby, then the *Polly*. Later came the sloop *Fame*. The schooners were the *Chatham, Sarah* and the *Eliza Kelley*. Another sloop running from Brewster was the *Rough and Ready*. The packets for the town of Harwich were the same as those for Chatham and Brewster with the signal telegraphs on hills denoting the arrivals and departures.

These photographs were taken at the saltworks on Wing's Island in West Brewster. The saltmills in the photo above appear to be in need of some repair as do the vats in the picture below. The photographs were probably made in the 1870's, just before the works were torn down. *Photos courtesy of the Brewster Historical Society.*

Above: The young ladies of the era display the styles in vogue at that time. The dresses are full length and not so much as an ankle shows but the crowning glory are the full flowered hats. **Below:** The Red Sea Balsam team came to Orleans and the photographer made a handsome picture for his album. The balsam was claimed to cure almost every malady for man or beast and could be used internally or externally. If you had an unknown ailment, it would probably cure it no matter what it was. *Photos by H. K. Cummings.*

Cape Cod had many assets, not the least of which were quiet towns with beautiful old homes, secluded wooded areas and pure white sandy beaches. The quiet town of Orleans, just east of Brewster, had many miles of shorefront on which to build saltworks. Historic Rock Harbor and Skaket Creek on Cape Cod Bay supported thousands of feet of working salt vats. Town Cove and Pleasant Bay afforded a large waterfront area for the industry. Namskaket was the name given the Orleans area by the Indians and it was the site of the first shipwreck on Cape Cod in 1626, when the Sparrowhawk was lost on Nauset Beach. The salt works were an important enterprise in the town. The number of superficial feet of saltworks at Orleans in the 1831 Massachusetts tax list was 897,035. In 1841 the number was reduced to 817,220 and in 1850 it was down to 63,400 which was similar to the rest of the Cape. The owners of saltworks were listed in Deyo's History:

"At the head of the Town cove Seth Smith had works, which were subsequently sold to Gideon S. Snow. On the northerly side between them and the Eastham line, were the works of Nathaniel Nickerson and of Jonathan Young, grandfather of D.L. Young. On the southerly side, in 1808, were in full blast the plants of Asa, Elisha and Josiah Hopkins, John Doane, Joseph and Isaac Seabury, and Daniel Higgins. Along the bay between Namskaket and Rock harbor were the works of Edward Jarvis, Blossom Rogers, Joseph Hurd, James Engles, Major Henry Knowles, Joseph G. Sloane, Captain Nathaniel Knowles, Jesse Snow, Captain William Smith, Sparrow Horton, Isaac Knowles, Sears Rogers, Josiah Freeman, Isaac Hopkins, Joseph Atwood, Seth Knowles, Edward, Edmund and Abiel Crosby, and William Myrick. In 1837, fifty plants made 21,780 bushels of salt. These after furnishing employment for a large number of men, gradually declined and but little salt was made after the middle of the century.

"East Orleans: The salt manufacturers here at an early day were: Lewis Doane, Joseph Crosby, Josiah Sparrow, Zoeth Taylor, Elkanah Linnell, who were located on Nauset harbor and Barley Neck; and William

The East mill was built circa 1800 and was used to grind rock salt from the evaporators into table seasoning. The mill was last worked in 1889 and then fell into disrepair. It was restored in 1960 and later sold to Heritage Plantation in Sandwich as an historic display. An electric motor was attached and today the mill demonstrates the fine art of grinding grain but using high voltage instead of wind power. The date of the photograph is listed as 1888. *Photo by H. K. Cummings.*

Myrick, who had a plant at the head of tide water near Lot Higgins Store. The windmill near there* was originally used for grinding salt.

"South Orleans: Salt was manufactured by the evaporation of sea water soon after the business had been commenced elsewhere. Thomas and Joseph Arey, Nathaniel and Thomas Gould, Asa and Adna Rogers, Thomas Mayo, John Kenrick, Henry Kendrick, Thomas Eldridge, Eliahim and Thomas Higgins were among the several who had plants around the ponds and coves of that territory."

*This is the East Mill which was moved from Orleans to Sandwich and became part of the exhibit at the Heritage Plantation.

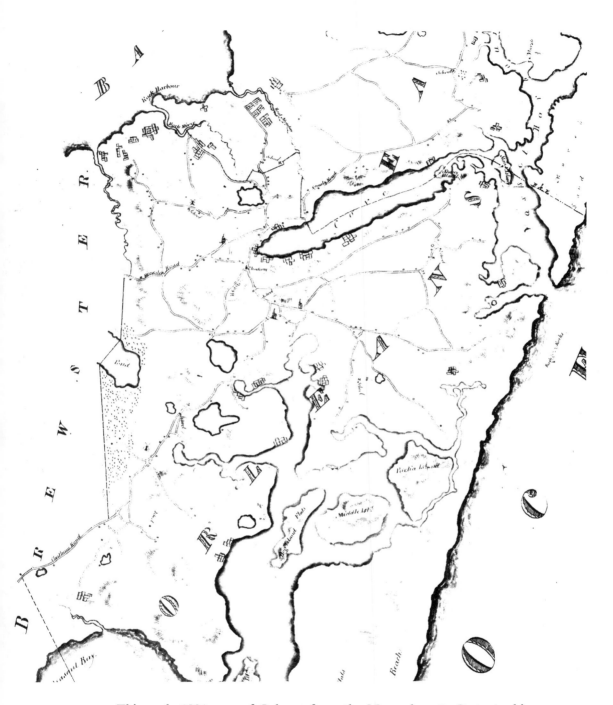

This early 1831 map of Orleans from the Massachusetts State Archives locates the saltworks around Town Cove, Rock Harbor and along Pleasant Bay.

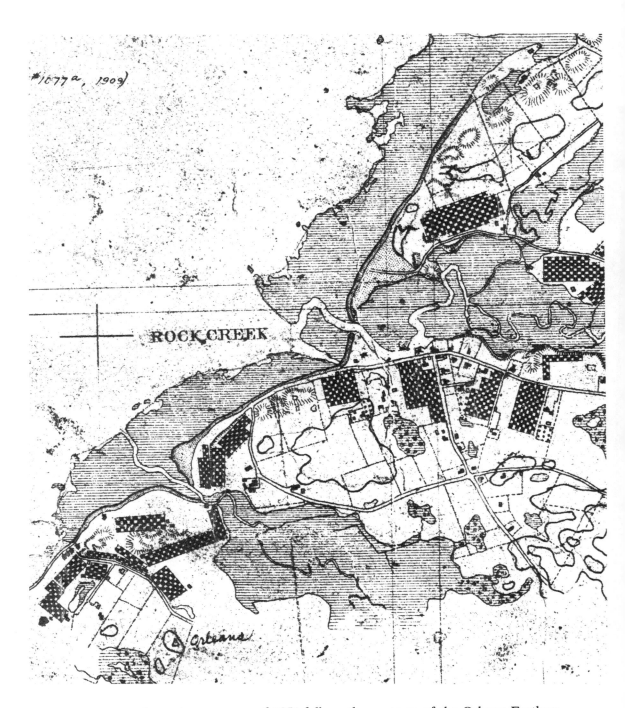

#1077a, 1909)

ROCK CREEK

Orleans

A coast survey map of 1851 follows the contours of the Orleans-Eastham Bay coastline and locates all of the saltworks in that area.

An aerial view of the Rock Harbor area as it looks today. The saltworks were torn down and many houses surround the former locations of the evaporators in Orleans and Eastham. *Aerial Photo by William P. Quinn.*

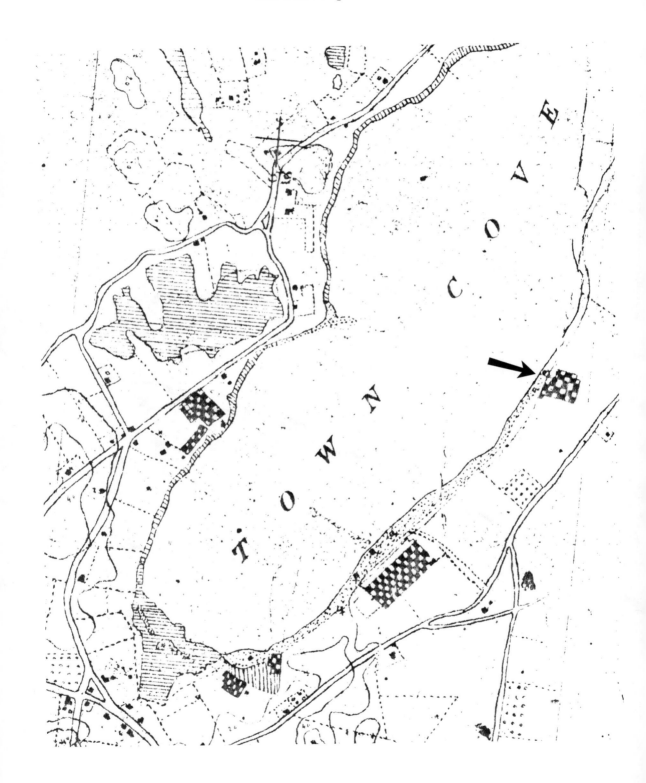

Opposite: The 1848 map of Orleans Town Cove locates several saltworks around the large body of water. **Above:** One of the saltworks was located in the Tonset section of Orleans and can be seen above, on the opposite shore, behind the house in the photograph. There is a salt mill near the water. The location is marked on the map with an arrow on the opposite page.

The commerce around Cape Cod was carried mostly by two-masted schooners very much like the drawing above. They were of 100 tons or less and were the workhorses of their era. *Drawing by Paul C. Morris, Nantucket, Mass.*

In Orleans, the sloop *De Wolfe* is the first packet named from this town in Deyo's History. There were earlier sloops on the run but the names were not known. The salt industry supported the early packets as outlined in Deyo's: "Not far from 1825, the need of better facilities for transporting their salt to Boston induced the manufacturers to encourage the construction of two schooners, and the *President Washington,* Captain Warren A. Kenrick, and *Lafayette,* Captain Jesse Snow, were built to accommodate the salt makers as well as the general traveling public." When the salt business began to decline, the schooners were sold and sloops replaced them. The vessels continuing in the packet service were the *Elizabeth, Emerald, Taglioni* and the *Harriet Maria* which was the last of the packets to run from Orleans to Boston. The loss of the *Emerald* on a Bay beach was reported in the Barnstable Patriot:

Above: Another example of an early homestead in Orleans. The vast acreage included grazing fields and farming lands. Lonnie's pond is on the left and was the location of two large saltworks in the 1830's.

"Nov. 11, 1847 - Loss of the sloop Emerald. - The packet sloop Emerald, Capt. Joseph Huckins, Jr., left Orleans, on Friday evening last, for this place, with the wind moderate. About an hour after her departure the wind blew up strong from the Northwest, and an attempt was made to put back. The wind continuing to increase, and the vessel making considerable water, she became unmanageable, and went on shore near the Breakwater at Dennis, and soon went to pieces. The Captain and crew succeeded in getting on shore in safety. The Emerald has been for many years employed as a packet between this port and Boston, but during the last two seasons she has run for the most part of the time to Provincetown. Little or nothing was saved form the wreck. No insurance."

The Assessors listing for the Town of Chatham for the year 1829, on page 160, lists Jesse Nickerson as owning 4,400 feet of saltworks. The men posing atop a salt mill might well be his heirs. *Photo from the Library of Congress, Washington, D.C.*

Chatham was located on the "elbow" of the Cape, south of Orleans and was another town with several miles of waterfront acreage to support saltworks. In 1831 Massachusetts tax lists, there were 1,457,690 superficial feet of works in this town. In 1841 the number was down slightly to 1,315,700 and in 1850 it was down further to 71,550. The owners of saltworks in this town were listed in Deyo's History:

"The earliest industry of the village - always excepting fishing - was the manufacture of salt, which soon after 1800 received considerable attention. These works, interspersed with flakes for drying fish, nearly covered the shore from the Sears' plant northeast of the village, southerly to the lights, around the shores of both ponds, and the rivers connecting them with the harbor. Enoch Howes, Henry Gorham, Elra Eldridge, Zenas Nickerson and Isaac Hardy had salt works on the beach east of the village; Joseph Loveland and Joshua Nickerson had extensive works east and south of Mill Pond; on the north side of Mitchell's river were the works of Joseph, John and Sears Atwood, and Micajah Howes, and at the head of the pond those of Isaiah Lewis; on the neck next to Stage harbor, those of William Hamilton, Christopher Taylor and Elisha, Joseph and Isaiah Harding; next west those of Thomas Smith; on the point next to Oyster pond those of Reuben Eldridge and Samuel Taylor; David Godfrey, Solomon Atwood and David Atwood on the south side of Oyster pond; Edward Kendrick and Nathaniel Snow on the north side of the pond; Collins Taylor and Benjamin Buck on the north side of the river; Nehemiah Doane and Samuel Doane east of these. Some of these works were in use until 1860.

"Chathamport: For salt manufacturing, the coves and bays of Chatham Port afforded the best of facilities, which were improved soon after 1800. Reuben Ryder is said to have first erected works on the shore of Pleasant Bay, and his sons, Isaiah and Christopher, continued them. The second was erected by Ensign Nickerson, sr. These were succeeded as rapidly as the works could be built by Kimble Ryder, his son Kimble Ryder, jr., Stephen Smith and his son - all on Ryder's river. Still later Ezra Crowell built extensive works on the same river and sold to Jonah and Joseph

Young, the latter being an early manufacturer elsewhere. Joshua Crowell, James Ryder and Captain Young soon established works, succeeded by Joseph, Rufus and Samuel H. Young. Edward Kent also erected works here. On Crowe's pond, in 1825, we find the works of Josiah Kendrick and Jonathan Eldridge; on Ryder's Cove the works of John Taylor and Reuben Snow; and further east, in the old harbor district, Myrick Nickerson made salt. Later still Ensign Nickerson, jr., the father of Orick and Samuel M., erected works on Crowe's pond; also on the bay side, which were continued until their decay in 1877. David H. Crowell confidently asserts that in 1835 around Ryder's cove he could count within sight twenty-eight wind mills for pumping brine. The only works standing in 1889 were those of Jesse Nickerson, who once owned eighteen hundred feet, and which were more or less used until 1886.

"North Chatham: From Myrick Nickerson's works on Ryder's river there were to the east of those of Prince Harding, John Ryder, Benjamin Dunbar, Joseph Taylor, Zenas Taylor and Salathiel Nickerson; at Old Harbor were those of Timothy Loveland, sr. - five thousand feet - Joshua Atkins, Allen Nickerson and Caleb Nickerson; and to the south of these the shore was lined with the works of Thomas Howes, Richard Nickerson and others; while well toward the village of Chatham were the extensive works of Richard Sears."

Most of the passenger business for the town of Chatham was carried on by the Brewster Packets *Chatham* and *Sarah*. The arrival and departure of these vessels was passed to Chatham by means of a signal telegraph on high hills between the two towns. The first packet vessel to run from Chatham was the *Canton*, Captain Barzillai Harding. Most of her business was in freight but a few passengers did travel on this vessel. Later others joined the business from Chatham. The *John J. Eaton, Eunice Johnson, C. Taylor, 3d* and the *P.M. Bonney*. There were a few others but most of the business was salt and produce cargoes.

The town of Chatham has had hundreds of shipwrecks along Chatham Bars and the carnage continues into present times. Above, the schooner *Grecian,* was wrecked there on December 6, 1885. The crew of five were rescued but the vessel was a total loss. *Photo from the collection of Joseph A. Nickerson, Chatham, Mass.* The wreck below occurred at sea but the hull washed ashore on Monomoy Island. The *Cora M.* came ashore on September 16, 1917 and was a total loss. The crew was rescued by the Coast Guard. *Photo courtesy of Noel Beyle, Eastham, Mass.*

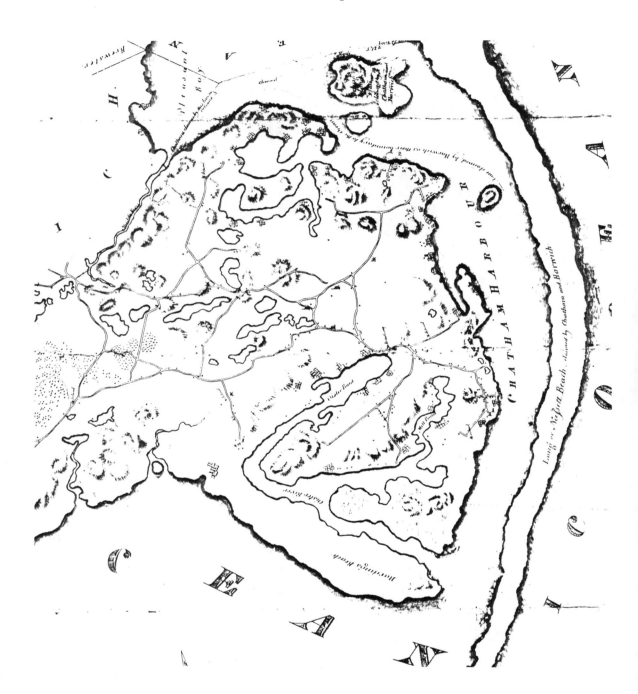

This map of Chatham was made in 1831 and locates the many different saltworks all over the town. The salt vats are represented on the map by several rectangular squares grouped together.

Above: This is an aerial photograph of Nickerson's Neck in North Chatham, located in the map on the previous page, was the location of many large salt evaporators. The Eastward Ho Country Club presently occupies much of this area today. Expensive summer cottages have replaced the saltworks everywhere else. *Aerial Photo by William P. Quinn.* **Below:** The Chatham Historical Society has a model of an early saltworks in their museum. It has two vats with roofs that move on rollers and a salt mill. *Photo from the Library of Congress, Washington, D.C.*

For the year 1829.

Joseph Atwood	2,400 Ft.	$ 1,111.
Sears Atwood	2,050	928.
Solomon Atwood	1,785	833.
David Atwood	1,230	595.
John Atwood	1,550	760.
Joshua Atkins	1,425	397.
Benjamin Buck	1,650	475.
Charles Briggs	1,000	287.
Isaiah Bee	575	313.
Joshua Crowell	2,000	719.
Jonah Crowell	2,871	892.
Samuel Doane	1,050	549.
Nehemiah Doane	1,050	549.
Benj. E. Dunbar	3,500	1,012.
Jonathan Eldredge	1,300	466.
Henry Eldredge	1,700	815.
Kimball Eldredge	800	435.
Levi Eldredge	800	435.
Gideon Eldredge	3,000	814.
John H. Edlredge	1,000	370.
Reuben Eldredge	750	310.
David Godfrey	750	390.
Henry Gorham	1,000	543.
Mulford Howes	2,000	1,084.
Micajah Howes	2,000	1,040.
Est. Thomas Howe	2,800	1,216.
Levi Harding	630	342.
Isaiah Harding	500	274.
Enoch Howes	1,000	542.
Isaac Harding	1,930	1,002.
Seth Harding	1,000	543.
John Hammond	700	384.
Est-P. Harding	2,050	741.
Elisha Harding	500	271.
Joseph Harding	1,050	551.
James Howes	950	515.
Edward Kent	1,000	315.
Edward Kendrick	1,000	542.
Josiah Kendrick	1,000	542.
Timothy Loveland	4,000	949.
Joseph Loveland	2,200	1,178.

Myrick Nickerson	2,229 Ft.	$ 847.
Selathiel Nickerson	2,800	1.051.
Richard Nickerson	2,850	967.
Lombard Nickerson	3,800	1,140.
Caleb Nickerson	4,500	1,402.
Est.Sim. Nickerson	2,620	844.
Joshua Nickerson	2,400	1,285.
Ensign Nickerson	6,476	2,971.
Jesse Nickerson	4,400	2,099.
Est-Ab. Nickerson	3,700	1,453.
Kimball Ryder	2,000	632.
Est.Kimball Ryder	2,700	855.
Est.Zenas Ryder	2,200	917.
Reuben Ryder	2,625	819.
Isaiah Ryder	1,930	493.
Christopher Ryder	2,700	928.
James Rider	2,000	836.
John Rider	1,750	396.
Richard Sears	1,075	341.
Esq. Richard Sears	2,050	632.
Thomas Smith	1,000	570.
Stephen Smith Jr.	1,000	577.
Stephen Smith	3,600	1,200.
Joseph Taylor	1,890	762.
Zenas Taylor	2,000	567.
Chris. Taylor, Jr.	1,550	864.
Samuel Taylor	1,000	520.
Reuben C. Taylor	500	273.
Est.-Rbn. C. Taylor	500	273.
John Taylor, Jr.	1,150	601.
Christopher Taylor	1,000	543.
Reuben Young	2,130	765.
Joseph Young	3,100	891.
Joseph Young, Jr.	1,630	637.
Samuel Young	630	342.
Rebeckah Rider	1,700	539.
Tabitha Harding	234	127.
Lurang Rider	700	303.

TOTAL............. 143,665 Ft. $ 57,291.

160

These two maps are taken from the 1851 coastal survey. They show a large group of saltworks on Chatham Harbor (upper) and another large collection on Mill Pond near the old light-houses in the lower map.

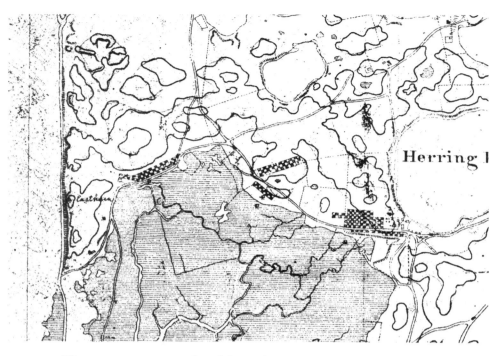

These two maps reproduced from the 1851 coastal survey show the bayside saltworks in Eastham. The upper group is off the great marsh north of Boat Meadow Creek while the lower heavier group of saltworks is south of the same creek.

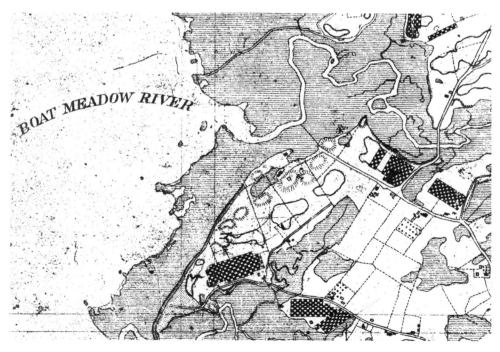

The Lower Cape Towns

In Eastham, the salt works were situated along the Bay shore and near the great marsh. There were several on the east side of the town near Town Cove and the Salt Pond. The 1831 Massachusetts tax lists Eastham as having 842,300 superficial feet. This number was reduced slightly in 1841 to 749,450. In 1850 the number was up to 770,000. The several inlets around the town facilitated the location of the works near the shores. Deyo's history listed the many owners of plants in Eastham:

"The works along the bay, commencing at the north side, were owned by Nathan F. and Elkanah Cobb, the latter selling his to Edward C. Clark; Joshua Higgins; Barnabas Mayo; George Collins; Peter Walker, who sold to E.C. Clark; Edward C. Clark; Deacon Benjamin Clark; George Clark; Timothy and Joshua Cole; Joshua and Seth Paine; Major Joel Snow; and Benjamin Walker. Around the north part of the Town cove and at Salt pond were: Herman S. Doane; Thomas Cobb; Michael and B.H.A. Collins; Geoge Seabury; Joshua Knowles, who sold to Joshua Cole; Samuel Knowles; Samuel Snow; Joshua and Seth Paine; William and Harding Knowles; and Barnabas Freeman. In all, the number of feet exceeded one hundred thousand, from whose evaporating vats were annually made large quantities of salt. As late as 1837 there were fifty-four plants yielding 22,370 bushels."

The oldest operating windmill on Cape Cod is in Eastham on Route 6 opposite the Town Hall. There are several legends as to the origin of this mill but it was reportedly built in Plymouth in the late 1600's and brought to Cape Cod on a raft during the late 1700's. After working for quite a few years, the mill was acquired by the town and is now a historic display on the Town Green. *Photo by Henry K. Cummings.*

One of the first packets listed from Eastham was in the 1820's, when Captain David C. Atwood began sailing the forty-ton sloop *Clipper* back and forth to Boston. It is not known if Capt. Atwood carried the legendary "first cargo of onions" but he might have, along with the passengers. Next was the *New York*, Captain Samuel Snow and after that the *Young Tell* with Captain Scooter Cobb. Others engaged on this route were the *A.C. Totten, Bay Queen* and *Flight.* In 1824, the sloop *Algerine*, Captain Jesse Collins carried salt to Boston at six cents per bushel. She was used only for freighting, not as a passenger vessel.

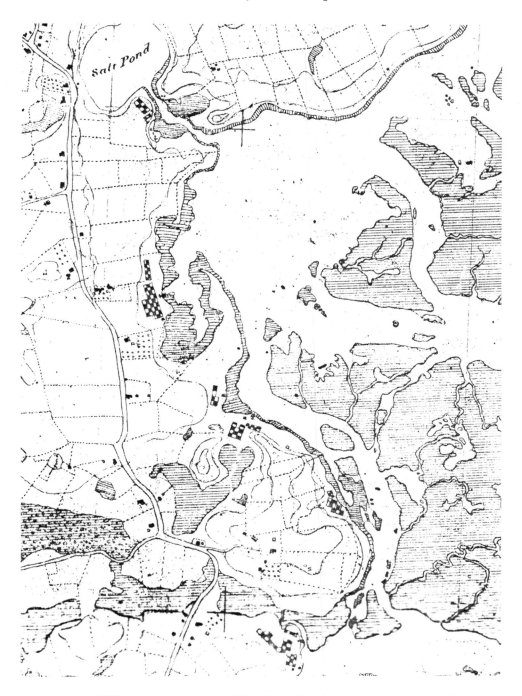

An 1851 coast survey map of Eastham locates several saltworks from the Town Cove all the way up to the Salt Pond.

A map from the coast survey of the center of the Town of Wellfleet shows several saltworks in operation at Wellfleet in 1850. There are also vats out on Chequesset Neck on the left side of the illustration.

Wellfleet was the next town north of Eastham and the saltworks here were not as extensive at the initial phase of manufacture in the County but they caught up. In 1821, a new company was formed. It was called "The Salt Manufacturing Company of Billingsgate" and had a capital of $50,000. The company carried the same name as the island in Cape Cod Bay off Wellfleet but it was not located there. A small colony occupied the island at that time. Parts of the island are today, just bare at low tide. The storms and tides slowly washed away this once busy fishing village. The island had several houses as well as a large brick lighthouse in the 19th century. In 1831, the superficial feet of saltworks on the Massachusetts tax rolls for the town of Wellfleet was 33,771. In 1841 it had multiplied to 319,500 feet but in 1850 the decline was marked by a reduction to 24,000 feet. The owners listed in Deyo's history were as follows:

"As early as 1800 the manufacture of salt by solar evaporation was commenced around Duck Creek and the bay shore of the village. East, in the cove, was the plant of Samuel Smith, and near Mr. Kemp's was that of Isaac Baker, afterward sold to David Atwood, who also owned others. Benjamin Witherell had works on the shore southwest and Amaziah Atwood's were where Timothy Daniels now resides. Deacon Whitman ran a plant in the neighborhood of Wells E. Kemp's, and Moses Dill's was opposite where Jeremiah Hawes resides. East of the last, where Warren Pierce resides, were the works of Freeman Bacon, which, after falling into the hands of Wells E. Kemp, were discontinued, and destroyed soon after. On the island south of Dill's plant was that of Stephen Bailey, and on the point adjoining the residence of E.I. Nye was Joseph Holbrook's. The long row of vats east of Jeremiah Hawes' residence once belonged to Henry Baker. On the bay Cornelius Hamblen also built and operated works."

Just after the War of 1812, three sloops began packet service between Wellfleet and Boston. The *Hannah, New Packet,* and *Mary* carried freight and passengers. The *New Packet* was lost on Minot's Ledge in a dense fog. She was replaced by the sloop *Pacific.* In the 1820's schooners took over from the sloops. The first was the *Swiftsure* commanded by Thomas Newcomb. Other schooners followed; the *Herald, Freemont,* and the *Merchant.* More schooners were built for packet service in the 1840's. The *Sophia Wiley,* and the *Golden Age,* joined the fleet. These were followed in the 1850's by the schooners *Lilla Rich* and *Nelly Baker.* Two more schooners were built in the 1880's, the *Freddie A. Higgins,* and the *J.H. Tripp.* These continued into the 1900's.

The town just north of Wellfleet is the town of Truro which had an active salt industry during the first half of the nineteenth century. In 1831 the Massachusetts tax rolls listed 611,800 superficial feet of saltworks here. In 1841, the number had dropped to 505,130 feet and in 1850 the footage had been reduced to 343,500. The several owners were listed in Deyo's History of Barnstable County:

"Among the first to manufacture was Dr. Jason Ayres, who erected works south of the pond at north Truro, which were subsequently owned by Samuel Coan. Captain Elisha Paine had works next to Coan on the south, and John Smith erected a plant next north, also purchasing that of John Grozier adjoining. Next north were the works of Edward Armstrong, and still further north, Colonel Joshua Small owned a plant which is said to have been the first in town. On the bay shore south of Elisha Paine's were the works of Sylvanus Nye, and adjoining were those of Jonah Stevens. On the north side of Little harbor meadows were located the works of Michael and Thomas Hopkins, the latter works passing into the possession of Doane Rich, who owned a plant on the south side of the meadows, and both of which were subsequently sold to Solomon Paine. South of Paine's were Reuben and Jesse Snow, and on the north of the Pamet River, near the present railroad depot, were the extensive works of Michael Snow. Along up the north side of Pamet River were Lewis Lombard, Ephraim D. Rich, John Kenney, David Lombard, Shubael Snow, David Smith, Elisha Paine, Levi Stevens, Hinks Gross, Jonathan Whorf, Joseph Collins, Freeman Atkins and Samuel Ryder. On the south side of the river, commencing near the depot, were Allen Hinckley, Michael Collins, Benjamin Hinckley and Leonard P. Baker; and further up the river, John Smith, Ephraim Baker and Solomon Davis. On the bay between Pamet river and South Truro, Elisha Newcomb had works, also Benjamin Hinckley; Perez Bangs' works were about half way between the river and South Truro, and Nehemiah Rich had a very extensive plant at the latter place. In 1837 Truro had 39 of these works, and the decline of the business commenced soon after."

The 1848 coast survey revealed a large concentration of saltworks along the Pamet River in Truro. There were many fishing vessels that sailed from this town and they required large quantities of salt to maintain their business.

The first packet to run from Truro was the pink *Comet,* Captain Zoheth Rich. It was followed by the same Capt. Rich sailing the *Postboy* back and forth to Boston. Later the vessels: *Young Tell, Mail* and the schooner *Modena* carried the freight and passengers to the city.

Above: In Provincetown, the first town hall was situated atop a high hill. This building burned down in later years and the location was used for construction of the Pilgrim Monument. *Photo courtesy of Cape Cod Photos, Orleans, Mass.* **Below:** The Provincetown waterfront in the late 1800's supported large areas of fish flakes. On the day this photo was made there appears the results of a fine catch. Many of the Provincetown fleet are in the background at anchor in the harbor. *Photo by Henry K. Cummings.*

At the tip of Cape Cod, Provincetown was the first landing place of the Pilgrims in 1620. This village was similar to the other towns except it was completely surrounded by water, with the exception of a narrow neck of land that connected it to the rest of the peninsula. In the early 1800's, salt was a major industry here. Those Cape towns with larger fishing fleets, needed a greater number of salt evaporators. Dennis, however, led all the towns with over two million feet of works but Provincetown had several acres of land covered with salt vats. John Warner Barber's 1840 illustration of the town's waterfront pictured many of the salt-mills along the shoreline. The spacious harbor could hold a fleet of ships and it was a favorite liberty port in the late 1800's and the early 1900's for the United States Navy. In 1837, there were 78 saltworks in Provincetown manufacturing almost 50,000 bushels a year. Some of these were located at out at Long Point and Race Point. At that time, there were large fish flakes along the inside shoreline to dry codfish for export. Several owners of saltworks were themselves fishermen. While the men were at sea, the wives tended the vats, the children and the house. As has been stated, "her work was never done."

In the early 1830's, Congressional funds were appropriated to conduct a survey of the town of Provincetown. The work was done during the years 1834-1836 and the result was a minute detailed map of the whole town. The map (on page 172) located every one of the saltworks and all of the salt mills. After the decline of the industry the saltworks boards were used to build all kinds of buildings around the town. There were houses and stores built with this lumber and several two-story fish houses along the shore which later became the studios of artists when that colony began at the Cape tip.

The list of salt works in Provincetown was impressive. In 1831, there were 145,795 superficial feet of works listed in the Massachusetts tax list. In 1841, the figure rose to 1,461,200 feet. After the business began a decline, the amount of footage was reduced to 791,000 in 1850. The assessed valuation of saltworks, per foot in 1841 was 1-2/3 cents. The valuation in 1850 was only one cent. This was probably an assessment figure at a fraction of their worth and may not represent the true value in dollars.

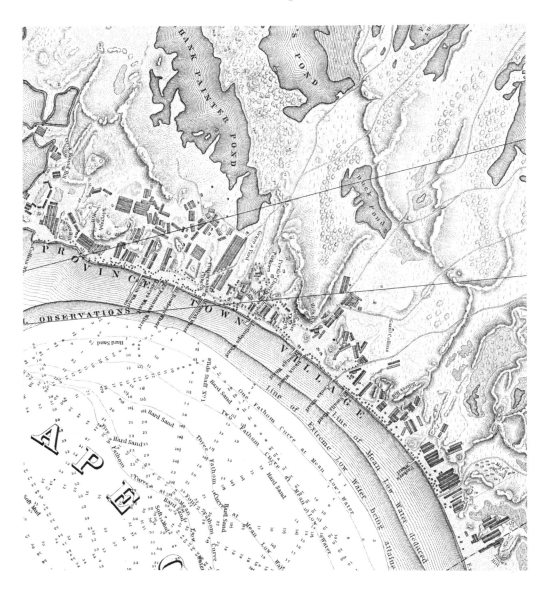

One of the most detailed maps to be made of a Cape Cod town was commissioned by the United States Congress in 1835. It was the village of Provincetown with part of Truro included. The above illustration is a small portion of the map and shows the central part of the town. The square dots along the shore represented the houses of the residents. The larger rectangles back from the shore were the saltworks.

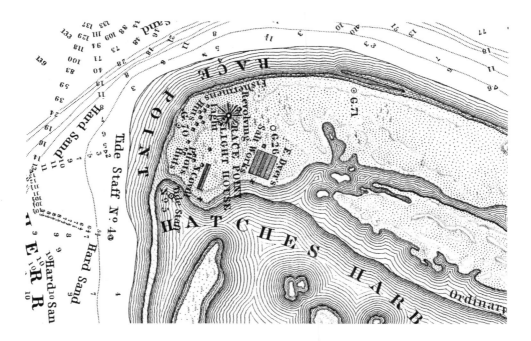

Above: Another small section of the map described on page 172 shows the detail of Race Point where the saltworks belonging to E. Dyers and N. Covill were located near the lighthouse. Other buildings at the point were huts for Boston Pilots and some fisherman's shacks near the beach. **Below:** Another section of the map located the saltworks at Long Point. This area was also the location of two forts that were built at the Cape tip during the Civil War but never fired a shot in anger.

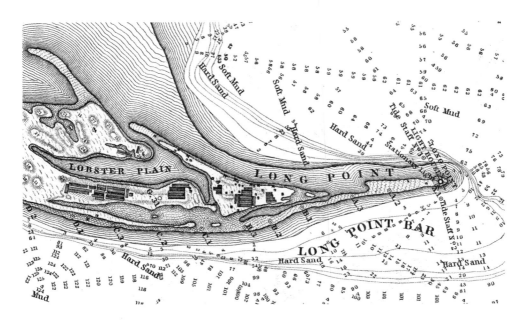

A report in the Barnstable Patriot on January 1, 1840 described a terrible storm which hit the Capt tip and damaged the salt works:

"Provincetown, Dec. 28th, 1839 - Last night and this morning we were visited with another violent gale of wind, which has done much more damage here than any former gale within the recollection of our oldest people. The loss of property cannot be estimated at less than $50,000., which principally falls upon the inhabitants of this town. The wind blew with great violence, causing the tide to rise much higher than usual, and nearly every vessel that was fastened at the wharves broke loose and drifted among the stores and dwellings along shore, demolishing everything in their way.

"About 20 salt mills were blown down and a vast quantity of salt works blown away. Many cellars of the dwelling houses were overflowed, and in some instances the inmates were compelled to leave their houses and seek shelter with their more fortunate neighbors. Some of the wharves were entirely swept away, and in fact our shores are piled up with fragments of wrecks, buildings, bbls of mackerel, lumber and spars."

Around 1820 the sloop *Truth* was the first packet to run between Provincetown and Boston. John Nickerson and his brother owned and ran her for several years along with the packets *Catherine* and *Packet.* In 1827, the sloop *Louisa* came to Provincetown under the direction of Captain Jonathan Cook. She was followed by the sloop *Osceola.* Others came along; the *Northern Light,* Captain Whitman W. Freeman, then the sloops *Sarah, Powhattan,* the schooners *Long Wharf, Waldron Holmes, Golden Age* and the *Nellie D. Vaughan.* There was competition from the steamers in Provincetown because of the deep harbor there. The *Naushon, Acorn, George Shattuck* and finally the *Longfellow* all made the run to Boston from Provincetown.

In 1849, a new clipper type schooner joined the fleet sailing from Provincetown to Boston. The *Melrose* was 125 gross tons and seventy-six feet long, the latest in arrangments and was very popular with the people of the town. The Yarmouth Register published a story about this vessel and Captain Cook on July 5, 1849. The story had originated in the Boston Atlas:

Maritime traffic continued around Cape Cod into the 20th century. The old sailing schooners came and went and would still be sailing today if there were cargoes without time limits. The sailing vessels had to relinquish their hold on the business to the more dependable steamers. The three masted schooner in the photograph, heavily laden with cargo was setting out with a good wind filling her sails.

THE PACKET SCHOONER MELROSE OF PROVINCETOWN

This beautiful clipper was built at Salisbury, on the Merrimac, by Messrs. W. & C. Burnham, under the superintendence of her commander, Capt. Cook. She is 60 feet long on the keel, 76 on deck - has 21 feet, 1 inch breadth of beam, 7 feet, 3 inches depth of hold, and measures 101 tons and 53/95ths. Her keel is of rock maple, 15 by 12 inches; the floor timbers 12 by 18; and keelson of the same dimensions as the keel. The floor timbers are bolted with seven-eighths of an inch copper through the keel; and the keelson is bolted through all, within an inch of the base of the keel, with inch iron. The ceiling on the floor is of 2-1/2 inches thickness, and the clamps of 3-1/2, square fastened with seven-eighths of an inch bolts driven through all, and riveted. Her planking on the bottom is of 2-1/2 inches, and on the bends, up to the covering board, it is all of 3-1/4 inches. Her frame, scantling, beams, and knees, are all of the very best seasoned white oak, and she is thoroughly copper fastened, well tree-nailed and ventilated. - As she is a packet, a large part of her is devoted to cabins; still she can stow below, and carry on deck, the bulk of 125 tons. Her bulwarks are 3 feet high, and she has a half poop deck 29 feet long, under which is the first cabin. It is entered from forward by a neat companion, and a staircase. It contains 14 berths, two water-closets, a pantry and a wash-room, and is tastefully painted in imitation of maple and oak, with walnut mouldings. It receives air through two stern windows and a large trunk skylight, 12 feet long by 3 wide and 2 high. The forward cabin is plain, but neat, it contains 22 berths and other arrangements for the comfort of passengers. Her deck is spacious, and well protected. Inside she is painted drab color, with a blue ribbon along the lower moulding of the rail; and outside, she has a white bottom, black bends and bulwarks, with a red moulding along the planksheer, and a white one along the rail.

Her masts rake 2-1/5 inches to the foot, and are 70 and 72 feet long. The foremast is 18-1/2 inches in diameter, and the main, 18 - bowsprit, 18 feet outward, and jibboom 14 feet outside of the cap. She has two topmasts, 18 feet long. Her lower masts are beautiful spars, bright as silver and smooth as glass. She is fore and aft rigged, and carries all the usual fore and aft sails. Her sails are of cotton duck, middle-seamed in the cloths, and set like boards. They were made by Mr. Alfred Adams, of Provincetown, and her spars were made by Mr. James Young, of Newburyport.

The model of the Melrose is truly beautiful. - She is very sharp forward, and has a fine dashy appearance. The whole rake of her stem is four feet, and of her sternport, 2 feet. Her bow has very little flare, but is carried up with great nicety and terminates in a raking billet-head, which is ornamented with gilded carved work. Her head boards are also ornamented with her name in gilded letters, and on her stern are a couple of gilded stars, between which is a carved and gilded eagle on the wing, bearing an olive branch in its talons. We have said that she was sharp forward, she is also clean aft, and her lines are truly rounded. - She has about two feet dead rise at half floor, and about 12 inches sheer. She is, as a whole, a very beautiful craft - sails fast, works well, and has fine accommodations for passengers. We congratulate the traveling community of Provincetown, upon having such a fine vessel for a packet. Her able commander, Capt. William Cook, is universally respected by all who know him. During many years he has been the regular Provincetown correspondent of the Boston press, and has always been distinguished for the accuracy and interest of his communications. Good luck to him and his beautiful clipper.

The Melrose runs between Provincetown and this port, and generally loads and discharges at City Wharf. - [Boston Atlas]

This photograph was taken in Provincetown in later years after the railroad came to town. The tracks were extended to the end of the pier but maritime trade continued in spite of the competition from the railroad. The ship arriving is a bark. Her crew were furling sails on the lower courses and the higher royals. She was probably getting ready to tie up at the pier. *Photo by Henry K. Cummings.*

The Decline of the Salt Works

Chapter Ten

The first half of the 19th century has been referred to as the "Golden Years" because of the prolific growth of industry during that period in the United States. Cape Cod commerce was nourished primarily by domestic coastal trading. New York City was one of New England's best markets during that era. Several different cargoes were traded, including cotton goods from Fall River, whale oil from New Bedford and Nantucket, and salt from Cape Cod. A large number of vessels hailed from the several towns on the Cape. Barnstable County boasted over ten thousand registered tons in 1815. By 1840, the total had grown to over fifty-six thousand tons and by 1860, just before the Civil War, the total tonnage from Barnstable was over sixty-three thousand tons. The average two-masted schooner measured about 100 tons.

During the growth of commerce in this period, large quantities of salt fish from Cape Cod went to to the West Indies and was traded for barrels of molasses. Most of the imported molasses was distilled into rum; millions of gallons of rum. There were other cargoes including lumber, lime and granite from other coastal ports in New England. A bold commercial experiment began in 1805 when Mr. Frederic Tudor of Boston shipped a cargo of 130 tons of ice to Martinique in the Caribbean. The ice was cut from frozen ponds during the winter and stored in ice-houses using sawdust and hay for insulation. Mr. Tudor continued to sell ice for several years. The perishable nature of the cargo sometimes resulted in a low profit

An illustration of the men of the Life Saving Service going to the aid of a stranded and broken vessel. The rigging is in shambles and the crew in the fore part of the ship awaiting rescue. This was typical work for the Life Savers in the late nineteenth century.

margin but over the years he prospered.

The maritime traffic rounding Cape Cod consisted mostly of coastal schooners and fishing boats. The sail to Boston from the Cape was a simple piece of navigation for the local captains but for vessels from other ports, passing Cape Cod in either direction was a challenge. Dangerous shoals waited for even the most experienced mariners. Vessels from New York on their way to the Grand Banks frequently sailed into Bass River to load with Cape Cod salts. They obtained both the white compound and men to help crew the ship. Accidents were common when the schooners passed over the shoals south of Cape Cod. The Monomoy wreckers did a good business refloating grounded vessels or salvaging valuable cargoes.

The Barnstable Patriot reported on one of the Cape's ship disasters in their April 22, 1851 issue:

"The 600 ton ship Columbus, of Newburyport, Capt. Balch, from Cadiz, 13th ult., with a cargo which included 3,500 hogsheads of salt, for Boston. She struck on the Bishop and Clerk Rocks, on Wednesday, and was driven over and went on the beach near Cotuit. The crew were saved in an exhausted state, and landed at Falmouth, and the ladies of that place learning of their destitution are deserving great praise for having immediately procured them clothing and money, sufficient to answer their present wants. Vessel and cargo will probably be a total loss, but the sails, rigging and anchors, it is thought will be saved. The Columbus was valued at $20,000, and was insured in Boston for $15,000, equally divided between the Boylston, Columbian and New England offices."

Above: The decline of the saltworks began in the 1840's and lasted into the 1880's when the final salt was made in Yarmouth and Barnstable. These works in Dennis show the vats falling into disrepair with the salvage of lumber the only avenue left for the owners. **Below:** The salt mills appear to be broken and no longer in use. Its too bad that someone didn't save one of these structures for posterity. *Photos by Henry K. Cummings.*

DECLINE OF THE SALTWORKS

In 1849, after Henry David Thoreau had traveled the length of Cape Cod, he arrived in Provincetown. His description of the saltworks in the town at that time was an abridged view of the dying industry: "The turtle-like sheds of the saltworks were crowded into every nook in the hills, immediately behind the town, and their now idle wind-mills lined the shore." Thoreau went on to describe the operations of the saltworks and finished the discourse with: "But they were now, as elsewhere on the Cape, breaking up their saltworks and selling them for lumber."

There were several factors that contributed to the demise of the salt manufacturing industry on Cape Cod. One of these was the repeal of Federal tariffs on foreign imports. The decline extended over a long period of time. But it was the influence a few particular events that brought about the end of a business that had contributed so much to the economy of the area during that prolific period in the nineteenth century. One item was the cost of soft pine from Maine. This wood was used almost exclusively in the construction and repair of the vats. The popularity of the product in other domestic markets increased its value. The rise in price made it uneconomical to continue its use on the Cape because the price per bushel paid to the salt makers varied from 40 to 60 cents. This small return precluded any decisions for repairs to damaged works. The state bounty was withdrawn in 1834. In 1838, there were proposals in Congress to reduce the import duty on salt. In the Massachusetts Legislature, resolves were passed advising our representatives to oppose these bills. The Massachusetts Senate passed a resolve "Concerning the Duty on Salt and the Bounty to Fishermen." This was enacted in 1839. (A copy of the resolves appears in the appendix.) A year later, the Massachusetts House passed a similar resolve but this did not stop the inevitable action by the United States Congress.

During the debate in the Congress, Massachusetts Senator John Davis pleaded with the assembly to consider the conditions that would result in the loss of the salt industry. Bounties and incentives had always

Above: J.W. Barber traveled the length of Massachusetts and wrote about every town he visited. He drew pictures of what he saw and this engraving of the waterfront at Provincetown is proved correct by the map on page 172. It has been widely reproduced in many publications. **Below:** The only salt vats on Cape Cod today are located at the Aptuxet Trading Post in Bourne. These two are not to scale as they are only 3 or 4 inches deep and that is not deep enough for any profitable operation. *Photo by William P. Quinn.*

been granted to sailors to encourage commerce and to maintain the fisheries as an apprenticeship for seamen who in time of war were reserve crews, ready to defend the country. Senator Davis related the experiences of the 1812 war and how skillful seamen from Massachusetts swelled the ranks of the U.S. Navy and how they won battles with efficiency and dispatch. The import duty by the Federal Government was reduced to 8 cents per bushel in 1842 and then reduced even further in 1846. The price of salt realized by the manufacturer dropped below fifty cents a bushel but this did not stop production entirely. Some of the remaining salt works on Cape Cod were operational well beyond the 1850's.

Since there were no new saltworks being constructed, no additional capital was needed and the evaporation process continued to produce salt at a very low cost. The manufacturing continued into the 1880's. When the older vats fell into disrepair, they were abandoned and taken apart but those still working continued. Storms, however, continued to take a toll on some of the unprotected vats. The Barnstable Patriot reported on a September storm in 1858:

"The Gale of Thursday last was the severest known in this section for many years - perhaps the severest within the memory of the present generation. A large amount of property was destroyed on the south side of the Cape, between Osterville and Chatham, partly by the high tides and partly by the wind. The principal damage was done to vessel in the harbors. In South Dennis, a large salt store, owned by Mr. Theophilus Nickerson, was removed from four to six feet from its foundation. Mr. Nickerson's salt works were literally all torn to pieces."

The Cape saltworks seemed to be able to go on forever and if the market had held, they might very well have continued. The brine was a natural preservative and the wooden vats might have been standing today had the demand for salt been maintained. When the profits declined and the return dropped below the cost of production, the saltworks were torn down. The lumber was used in construction of buildings or any other project that needed boards, even some homes. Probably the chief reason for the decline was the increased competition from the salt springs in New York, Virginia and Kentucky. An article printed in the Barnstable Patriot on Saturday, September 4, 1830 described the salt mines in New York:

"Salt Manufacture."

"It is generally known to the public of this County that immense quantities of salt are manufactured in York State. (New York) But the exact location of the springs, and the method of procuring the salt is not known to a certainty by all. Having enjoyed the pleasure of viewing the works, we can give an imperfect sketch of them for the information of those who are interested in this extensive manufacture. The Salt Springs are in the towns of Liverpool, Salina and Syracuse in the County of Onondaga. There are also extensive springs in 'Onondaga hollow' so called by the Yorkers. About 700,000 bushels are said to have been made in the town of Salina, in one year, 400,000 in Liverpool and in Syracuse.

"The works which we had an opportunity of examining in Syracuse, are constructed upon the plan of the works upon the Cape and on our own coasts and beaches - Open and extensive vats, covered at night and during the rainy and wet weather. But evaporation is hastened by boiling the water in large kettles constructed on purpose, in Liverpool and Salina. Wood is abundant and so cheap, that the expense is very trifling, the water is drawn up by horses and steam power, and it is estimated that 90 gallons of water will make one bushel of salt, so perfectly is the water saturated with salt.

"In Syracuse, the works which are very extensive, probably one half mile in a continued range, are on the border or outskirts of the town, on the South-west side of the road from Auburn to Syracuse, as the stage goes into the town it passes by and between the works. Should these Salt springs continue inexhaustible, as they probably are, a town equal in size to any of our New England cities will soon arise on that excellent tract of land, 'Onondaga hollow.' The fever and ague prevails to a considerable extent in the summer and fall months otherwise it would be a very desirable residence to our New England farmers, and as healthy as any of our country towns, as the fever and ague prevents the existence of consumption in the system."

The article was probably not reviewed with any great enthusiasm by the people of Cape Cod engaged in the manufacture of salt but the message was clear. Competition was coming nearer and the opening of the Erie Canal in New York on October 26, 1825 certainly improved the market for salt produced in that state. The canal passed very near Syracuse and this enabled salt manufacturers there to ship their cargo to New York City at a much lower cost. Gradually the saltworks began to vanish from the Cape Cod landscape. It was a slow change but over the years they disappeared and nothing was built in their place along the wide expanse on the shoreline. They were picturesque as well as functional and many artists set them on canvas. In later years, the invention of photography was developed just in time to record their existance on film. Most of the photographs, however, are of works which had been abandoned and were no longer in use. Some, however, show the vats with water still being evaporated.

Quite often, Cape Cod's northeast storms did great damage to the saltworks. High winds moved the roofs off the vats and broke the wooden structures beyond repair. The remaining wood ended up being burned for kindling or, more often it was used in building. This practice was carried out albeit with much consternation of the local carpenters becuse the saltworks boards badly oxidized their metal tools. The lumber, however, was almost indestructible and guaranteed to last forever because, over the years, it had been steeped in brine, but it would not hold paint. There are numerous barns, outbuildings and houses on Cape Cod today constructed with wood from the saltworks. The wood is a hoary white and still salty. All of the nail holes are rusty. Many old buildings in Yarmouth have boards still weeping salt, over a hundred and fifty years after having been dismantled. Some of this lumber was from twenty to thirty inches in width.

At the beginning of the season in 1842, a convention was called for all of the salt-makers on Cape Cod. A notice in the Barnstable Patriot read:

"A meeting of salt manufactures, without distinction of party, will be held at Higgins Hotel in Orleans on Tuesday, the 12th of April at 10 o'clock a.m. It is recommended that the manufacturers in each town choose as many delegates as they think proper to attend the Convention.

"The object of this meeting is to take such measures as the manufacturers may think proper, to protect their interests in the approaching revision of the tariff. We hope the citizens of Barnstable County, interested in this important branch of business, will promptly respond to the call thus made upon them. Prompt and united action alone, can prevent the prostration of one of the means by which we live."

The announcement was signed by John Reed, Loring Crocker, Edward Thacher, Nathan Crocker, Leonard Hopkins, Alvin Howes, Orren Howes, Uriah Howes, Geo. Howes, Daniel Howes, David Crowell, Andrews Hallet, James Smith, Oliver Hallet, Isaiah Crowell, Goege Wing, Nathan F. Sears, Gamaliel Howes, Alex Howes, Peter Hall, Ebenezer Paddock and Isaac Crowell. Not coincidently, these names are listed in the early tax rolls as owners of saltworks on Cape Cod. The meeting was well attended and officers were elected for the organization. The president was John Reed of Yarmouth. Vice presidents were: Gen. Elijah Cobb of Brewster, Solomon Davis of Truro, Oliver C. Swift of Falmouth and Seth Crowell of Dennis. The results of the meeting produced a list of eight resolutions to be forwarded to the Federal Congress in Washington. This may have helped as the tariff was maintained for a few more years.

After 1837, salt production began a sharp decline and by 1845, it had been reduced by half. It is probably safe to assume that there were different levels of quality in the manufacture of salt. Loring Crocker of Barnstable won an award for purity in the salt he made. An article in the Yarmouth Register on October 28, 1847 attested to this fact:

"SALT: - Amoung the articles exhibited at the Cattle Show and Fair were a box of coarse and another of fine salt, manufactured by Messrs. Loring & Nathan Crocker, of Barnstable. The late Mr. Loring Crocker had the reputation of being the best salt manufacturer in the county, and his sons have not departed from the way in which they were trained up.

"The coarse was a selected specimen. The crystals were large and beautiful, and the article was as pure and strong as was ever manufactured.

"The fine salt was a fair sample of the article manufactured by them. It was very fine, white and pure, and a superior article for the table or the dairyman.

"The Crockers have recently erected a fine salt mill, with all the necessary fixtures and machinery for drying, grinding and putting it into bags. The salt ground by them is of their own manufacture, and is free from lime, the salts of the bittern, are carefully washed in new brine from all impurities. There are others as careful and well skilled in the manufacture as the Crockers, but those who purchase their salt will be certain of obtaining a first rate article."

There is no question that, those making a higher grade of salt stayed in business longer than those turning out an inferior grade. Production continued, however, as did the damage from storms. In the gale of April, 1851, it was reported in the Barnstable Patriot that: "Loring and Nathan Crocker lost about 500 bushels of salt by the tide flowing into their salt houses and some of their salt works were carried across Mill creek into the garden of O.G. Woodbury."

Production was not halted completely as was discovered in a ledger book at the Sturgis Library at Barnstable. The accounts from the Crocker partnership at Barnstable revealed that several hundred bushels of salt were sold to fishing vessels and others from 1856 to 1868. In the 1860's there were sales of 800 bushels of salt sold on ten different occasions and other smaller transactions totaling in excess of eight thousand bushels. On April 20, 1862 the book shows that 680 bushels of salt were delivered on board the schooner *Flora*. Another entry in the ledger in December, 1868 and January 1869 shows different sales of 75 to 100 bushels at prices of sixty cents per bushel. It is apparent that at that time, the price of Cape Cod salt for fishermen was still cheaper than the foreign import because of duties that were levied.

The town of Truro had a large number of saltworks along the shores of Pamet River. Shebnah Rich wrote in his book about Truro:

"Truro was well situated for saltworks, and was a ready market for all that could be made. All along the shores and the banks of Pamet, its arms and coves and points were well covered, and every breezy summit was crowned with a picturesque windmill."

Because of the extensive saltworks in Truro, a large fleet of fishing and packet vessels used Pamet Harbor. After some delay, in 1849, the Government erected a lighthouse at the entrance to the harbor at what was called "Snow's Beach." The light structure was placed atop a house and was only used for a few years. The saltworks in Truro was a profitable business but at the outset of the decline, production dropped off sharply. This lighthouse was discontinued in 1856. The other lights in Cape Cod Bay were Billingsgate in Wellfleet and Sandy Neck in Barnstable. There was a movement to re-establish the light in 1858 by those fishermen using the navigational aid but the Lighthouse Board in Washington took no action.

In 1865, less than one hundred thousand bushels of salt were made on Cape Cod and manufacturing dropped steadily after that until the end came at Yarmouth in 1888. One reason this town held on the longest was its protected location for saltworks on Bass River. Another reason was the production of medicinal salts and magnesium sulfate. A magnesia factory was built in 1850 at Yarmouth near the waterfront. It burned down two years later. A second factory was built on the site of the first and this business was carried on until the end of the salt production. The saltworks supplied the raw materials for the magnesia plant. There are no remains of the large area of saltworks even here in Yarmouth. The little evidence we have to prove they were here are photographs made in the late 1800's and the old boards still weeping salt inside some of the Cape Cod barns and sheds.

Another article printed in the Barnstable Patriot, dated March 9, 1860 raised the hopes some of the salt-makers. It was small help to the dying industry and the coming conflict probably arrested the promotion for good. The article stated:

"Interesting To Salt Manufacturers. We learn that Capt. James Taylor of South Dartmouth, has applied for letters patent for an important discovery respecting *bitter water,* hitherto used in connection with Taylor's Tree Protector. The great cheapness of this agent, together with its peculiar properties of non-evaporation, resistance to cold, &c., commended for purposes to which hitherto more expensive and less perfectly adapted liquids have been applied. We have noticed with some concern the gradual demolition of some of the Saltworks in this vicinity. We have been favored with an explanation of Captain Taylor's new application, and we would take the liberty of advising all interested in Saltworks to be of good cheer, for in our opinion 'a good time is coming.' If this discovery of Taylor's succeeds, which seems highly probable from experiments already made, it may not be too much to say that the manufacture of bitter water will pay, and the salt made will be clear gain."

To exacerbate the situation was not uncommon in those days. It was like rubbing salt into a wound. The Commonwealth of Massachusetts issued publications periodically and one was published at this time period to bring happiness to the predictors of doom. The California gold rush was going strong at this period and it was the *State Record and Yearbook of General Information* for the year 1850. It is possible that the gradual decline of the saltworks industry on Cape Cod contributed to this report:

BUSINESS OF MANAGEMENT

"To review the business of the Commonwealth, in a manner that should prove in any degree profitable to our readers, would require many pages, - more space than our limited work affords for a single topic. We can do but little more than make general references, leaving each one to pursue that course of inquiry best suited to his taste or interests.

"Our citizens, of all classes, report their usual diversity of results. Some are satisfied, some are disappointed. Some have added to their worldly means, but have impoverished their souls; while others have failed to improve either their wealth or their conscience. Some have become poor by misfortune, some by imprudence, some by wickedness, and some by indolence. Some have *continued* poor in spirit, while they have increased their riches; while others have continued rich, who have no wealth but the wealth of good deeds.

"The number of failures from Dec. 15th, 1848, to January, 1850, returned to the office of the Secretary of the Commonwealth by the Commissioners of Insolvency, is 520. Of these 105 were in the city of Boston. The number from Oct. 1, 1847, to Dec. 15, 1848, was 1,274 - making in all 1,794, - 451 of which were in Boston.

"The rapid emigration of our citizens to California is a striking feature of the times. Thousands have left us with high expectations of sudden wealth, and if they are not taught anew the old maxim, that *"all is not gold that glitters,"* many of them will be called upon to realize a more important truth - *that most that is good is not gold.* A man may succeed in accumulating gold, but he may not be able to keep it for legitimate ends. He may indeed gain the precious metals, and lose, by a mistaken reliance upon them, what is by far more precious - his character. He may become a man of money, and exchange a life of industry for one of indolence, a life of honest simplicity for one of dissipation. Such an exchange, on any terms, becomes the source of transgression and misery, and is more to be dreaded than any plague to which the body is liable.

"The number of vessels that have cleared at Boston for California during the past year is 151, as follows:-ships 58; barks 37; brigs 41; schooners 15."

Near the end of the boom, just prior to the Civil War, the 1860 business directory for New England contained a variety of enterprises, most of which are obsolete today. The list included candlestick manufacturers, carriage, coach and sleigh builders, sleigh bell manufacturers, coopers (wooden barrel & box makers), tanneries, daguerreotypists (early photographers), gas light companies, gristmill builders, millstone manufacturers, harness makers, hoop skirt manufacturers, blacksmiths, whitesmiths (tinsmiths), ice dealers, liniment manufacturers, sailing packet agents, quarriers (stone cutters), ship's riggers, sail makers, dead eye makers and wagon manufacturers. Most of these entrepreneurs have faded into history and a large portion of their machinery was either taken apart or abandoned. One important Cape industry in the late 1800's was the manufacture of ladies hats. Seagull feathers were used to trim the bonnets and thousands of these birds were killed as well as several other of the species. It wasn't until after 1900 that laws were passed to protect the birds.

In 1859, Edwin L. Drake was successfull while drilling for oil in Titusville, Pennsylvania and the petroleum industry was born. The crude oil pumped out of the ground, when refined, produced a better fuel for illuminating lamps in the home (and lighthouses). Kerosene burned brighter and with less odor. Its popularity spread rapidly and this change succeeded in extinguishing most of the sperm oil lamps all over the country. There were other products from the oil industry including more efficient lubricants for machinery and axle grease for wagons. At this period there were several industries in decline. Many of the American whaling vessels were left to rot at their piers but this, unfortunately, did not stop the slaughter of whales. Advancing technology was responsible for the demise of several other 19th century professions. The steam engine and cars on iron rails contributed to a reduction in the number of coasters and packet boats around New England. These vessels nearly disappeared completely in the early 1900's. There were, however, a few who would not quit. Some of these men owned their own boats and continued to sail between southern New England ports. The overhead was minimal and an occasional cargo of freight kept them going.

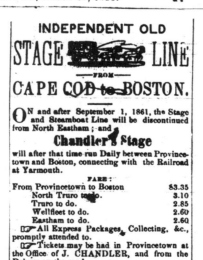
The Barnstable Patriot and the Yarmouth Register carried advertisements for transportation to and from Cape Cod through the years beginning with the packet schooners and stage coaches and then for the railroads. One interesting ad in 1868 was for both the railroad and packet schooner in the same column.

The first train to arrive in Orleans was in 1865 and this photograph was supposed to be a record made on that day. There is a difference of opinion on this and it may or may not be a true picture of that event as it occurred.

A couple of the better known engines on the Cape Cod run were the Highland Light and the Old Colony No. 186.

The remaining evidence of 19th century industries faded into oblivion. The fulling mills, tanneries and saltworks all disappeared along with the evidence of their existance. There are no crumpled foundations of salt-vats left today. We are fortunate that someone was perceptive enough to record a few of them on film for posterity. During the second half of the eighteenth century, the railroad was the catalyst for an industrial revolution that spread far and wide along the entire eastern seaboard. This opened up broad markets heretofore unavailable to Cape Cod products. But with limited production capabilities, the Cape could not compete with the larger industrialized cities in New England.

Salt played an important part in the Civil War, fought in the United States between April 15, 1861 and April 9, 1865. The north held the advantage over the south in finances, agriculture, population and manufacturing. A blockade was set up around all the seaports in the south and the salt stocks in the Confederacy ran low. The southern troops lived mostly on pork, and salt to preserve it was in short supply. The Confederate States set up a saltworks on the west coast of Florida but troops from the north staged a raid and smashed it. Salt did not win the war for the Northern states but it did influence the outcome.

The industrial history of Massachusetts industry is wide and varied. In the second half of the nineteenth century, there was a large shoe industry in Lynn, This activity spread rapidly to other towns after the manufacture of shoe machinery was introduced. There were several small towns that prospered greatly from this work: Abington, Hopkington, Marlborough, Milford, Natick, North Bridgewater, North Brookfield and Spencer are but a few of the municipalities that underwent expansion, making boots and shoes. There were other industries in the state making cotton and woolen goods, in the towns of Adams, Blackstone, Chicopee, Clinton Fall River, Holyoke, Lawrence, and Lowell. Industry on Cape Cod was again changing at this time. The harvesting of cranberries had become a profitable business and summer visitors were coming to the Cape in increasing numbers. In the latter part of the 19th century, because of the increasing influx of people, there were several cottage colonies constructed along the shores of Cape

Above: The packet steamer *Longfellow* was named after the famous poet. She was 413 tons and carried on the service between Provincetown and Boston from 1883 until 1903. She was wrecked off Cape Cod in September, 1904. **Below:** The *Cape Cod* replaced the *Longfellow* and remained on the Boston run for several years.

Cod using lumber from the old saltworks. In some cases, the foundation posts for the saltworks became the foundation posts for the cottages.

Machinery for the various trades was manufactured in several Massachusetts cities and towns. Many smaller towns grew larger and thrived with their diverse industries. Some of the more important manufacturers made boxes, chairs, cutlery, dye-stuffs, glass, hosiery, matches, medicines, nails, pencils, pianos, sewing machines, steam engines and women's bonnets. The creative geniuses, in partnership with the developing capitalists, enhanced the financial status of the people in the Commonwealth. The value of manufactured goods in Massachusetts in the 1870's exceeded two hundred million dollars annually. The success of their businesses brought about a higher standard of living for the various classes of society. One result of this was increased recognition of the arts and sciences. Educational institutions flourished along with the economic health of the state and prosperity abounded.

There were some men of the sea from Cape Cod who left to make their fortunes elsewhere. Edward Knight Collins from Truro founded an Atlantic steamship line to rival the English Cunard steamers in 1852. The American line established luxury in overseas travel. The Collins line carried more passengers than its competition but tragedy struck when two of the ships were lost at sea with a heavy loss of life. The line went bankrupt after only five years of operation. Lorenzo Dow Baker from Wellfleet was eminently more successful. In 1871, he gambled with a cargo of bananas from Jamaica to Boston in a sailing vessel. With a little luck and fair winds he succeeded in his venture and sold his cargo at a handsome profit. He proceeded to establish the Boston Fruit Company. Over a period of twenty years the business expanded and later became the United Fruit Company. This company's fleet grew to over one hundred ships carrying bananas from the Caribbean to the United States.

In the seventeenth century, communications on Cape Cod began along the early Indian trails. The present route 6A highway winding between Eastham and Sandwich was originally one of these byways. Roads were carved out of those rude paths and later freight wagons were

The train first came to Provincetown in 1873. This station was located on Bradford Street and the tracks extended through to Commercial street and out on the pier. The houses on the right side of the photograph are still in their same location today. *Photo courtesy of Cape Cod Photos, Orleans, Mass.*

introduced, transporting goods and carrying the mails. The public was invited to ride in the early nineteenth century as stage coaches traveled the Post Roads between large cities in Massachusetts. But packet boat travel between coastal ports continued to be popular, where available, especially for Cape Codders. There was an ample number of passengers on both the stage coaches and the packets. Those who did not trust water travel were welcome aboard the coaches.

As the industrial growth spread in New England, canals in the interior part of the state helped to carry barge-loads of goods from one city to another. Mail began on Cape Cod as early as 1790 when a rider on horseback made the trip to and from Boston once a week to carry letters. The Government mail service expanded rapidly and by the 1830's daily service was instituted on the Cape. The Post-Rider was always a welcome visitor to the several villages and towns. The stage coaches took over delivery from the Post-Riders and later, the contract was awarded to the railroads. Ultimately, steam engines pulled mail cars to every town on the Cape. Today all the mail is delivered over the highways by trucks.

The development of steam power occurred early in the early nineteenth century. An ingenious experiment by a man named Stephenson in England, using steam power on a railroad, ultimately resulted in development of the concept. The existance of a large industrial base was the motive for the inevitable spread of this new transportation network throughout the Commonwealth of Massachusetts. A map of the iron rails leaving Boston resembled a spider's web in most all directions and by 1850 the public could travel to other states on the train. The road was extended to Plymouth in 1845 and was completed to Provincetown by 1873. At that time, 1,657 miles of railroad had been completed in Massachusetts. During the last days of the salt industry, some of the bushels of salt manufactured here were carried on the freight trains.

Later, with street railways in all of the major cities, unlimited travel was available and affordable for the common man. There were, additionally, luxurious accommodations for the carriage trade. The construction of the railroads also brought communications by wire. Telegraph lines were erected alongside the railroads and it was possible to send messages all over the state. The expanded rail service opened wider markets for the freight shipper and his products. Cargoes were carried across the state and thence over the ocean at a greater speed than ever before. Just after the Civil War, in 1869, a trans-Atlantic undersea cable was landed at St. Pierre-Miquelon. These are two small islands owned by France, just south of Newfoundland. Soon, another cable was laid to Duxbury, Massachusetts, thus completing a communications link between New England and Europe. In 1879, the French Atlantic Cable landed a direct cable from Brest, France, to Eastham, on Cape Cod. The cable, was moved to another building at Orleans in 1890. It operated until 1959 when it was replaced by modern communications.

The oceans provide a myriad of treasures. The harvest of fish continues to be the greatest gift for mankind. The Cape Cod saltworks is another example in the early part of the nineteenth century. Mr. Phineas T. Barnams statement that "There is a sucker born every minute," was proved beyond a doubt when two con-men used the ocean waters to hoodwink some very rich investers. There are various get-rich schemes presented to the public every day. The early alchemists tried to turn lead into gold but failed. Today, sea water is turned into a form of gold, (fresh water) in the Middle-East Arab world by desalinization for a public water supply in the desert countries. These operations are just the opposite of saltworks.

In the latter part of the 19th century an elaborate scam called the "Lubec Klondike Caper" was revealed down east in Maine where gold was supposedly extracted from ocean water by means of a wondrous machine. Lubec is next door to Eastport and is conveniently far removed from the big cities from where the investers were lured. The remote location was an integral part of the plan. In early 1898, two men, Charles Fisher from Martha's Vineyard and the Reverend Prescott Jernegan of Middletown, Massachusetts, got off the Boston boat at Lubec and took rooms at the best hotel in town, the Lubec Inn. What better assurance of propriety than to have a minister as a partner. In a few days, the scam started with the purchase of an old tide mill near the town. They hired local labor to set up the intricate machinery to extract gold from seawater.

The Alaska gold rush was quite popular at this time and gold-fever was sweeping the country. The new firm was called: "Electrolytics Marine Salts Company," and they invited investers from New York and Boston to view the new machinery in action. And they came, of course, to look and be convinced of the validity of the process. After viewing the machinery, they left with a small amount of gold dust (24 carat) to be assayed. The word got around fast and investors poured millions into the new company. The stock sold for one dollar per share and over a period of less than one year, over nine million shares were sold. Still the investors came, saw, and bought into the company. Fisher, of course, was an expert diver. He *"salted"* the underwater machinery every night with gold dust for the next group of investers to see. These wealthy men were invited into the plant and the machinery was raised out of the water. Upon close inspection, particles of gold were found scattered along the bottom shelf. This was scooped up, dried and passed out to the gullible investors. When their supply of gold dust ran out, so did Fisher and Jernegan. At this time, the newspapers were asking too many questions about the secret process of the special machines. A few days later, both men disappeared from the little town of Lubec. Along with Fisher and Jernegan went the nine million dollars. All the victims had left were some fancy stock certificates. They were not even valued as souvenirs.

A typical Cape Cod saltworks in the later part of the nineteenth century. These works were situated on Wing's Island in West Brewster. The saltworks appear to be in disrepair which would date the photograph in the late 1880's. *Photo courtesy of The Brewster Historical Society, Brewster, Massachusetts.*

Epilogue

The research for *The Saltworks of Historic Cape Cod* has been an interesting and, at times, a challenging task. Most of the known information about this early industry is sparse and scattered throughout the several historic publications concerning Barnstable County. I found different entries recorded about Captain John Sears and the saltworks development in East Dennis. It is often difficult to narrow down a two-hundred year old story with any degree of accuracy. The Sears genealogy supported most of the information uncovered during the research and there are members of the Sears family, still living today, in East Dennis near where Captain Sears began his first experiments.

During the research, it was discovered that the editors of the two Cape Cod weekly newspapers; the Yarmouth Register and the Barnstable Patriot, waged a continuing battle of words in their columns every week. The motive for this was, they were politically opposed. The news about Cape Cod saltworks was very limited in these publications even though it was one of the more important industries of Barnstable County. The story of the beginning and development of the evaporators on the Cape was not mentioned in the newspapers of that era. It was as though they didn't exist. The price lists of commodities included salt from overseas but none from the Cape Cod manufacturers.

Probably the most satisfaction from doing this book was the chance to learn more about the delightful history of Colonial Cape Cod. The fact that most of the people would rather ride the packet boats over the stage coaches was unique and the stories told of that type of transportation were at times fascinating. It is hoped that the reader has perused the book with as much pleasure as I enjoyed doing the research.

W.P.Q.

This photograph was taken in Provincetown about 1905. There were no saltworks visible in the picture as by this time they had all been torn down. Most of the wood was used to build houses, barns and sheds. Many of these structures in the foreground were probably made with the lumber from the abandoned saltworks. *Photo courtesy of Cape Cod Photos, Orleans, Mass.*

APPENDIX

The Appendix contains some interesting papers about the Saltworks of Cape Cod. The first is a copy of a letter, dated September 30, 1814, from Captain Richard Raggot of the British Frigate *Spencer*, to the Selectmen of Orleans. The letter demanded payment of one thousand dollars to protect the saltworks of the town. The original document has been preserved and is on display at the Orleans Historical Society.

The next paper is an article from the Barnstable Patriot dated Nov. 30, 1858 with a story on the decline of the saltworks and a short history of their early development with a copy of the patent awarded to Captain John Sears. The patent was dated January 24, 1799 and was signed by John Adams. This is followed by an obligation from John Sears to Nathaniel Freeman for rights to build saltworks in three outer Cape Cod towns. The original Sears document is in the possession of the Dennis Historical Society. Another paper by Nathaniel Freeman is an obligation to Reuben Ryder of Chatham giving him the right to build saltworks in Chatham.

The next paper is by Doctor James Thacher, dated August 16, 1802. The dissertation covers his observations on Cape Cod Saltworks and the technology employed in the manufacture of salt. The final paper is a copy of A bill passed by the House of Representatives of the Commonwealth of Massachusetts and is dated January 4, 1840. This resolve requested the Congressmen representing Massachusetts to oppose the passage of a bill repealing the duty on imported salt.

Copy of a letter sent to Orleans Selectmen by Capt. Raggot.

His Britannick Majesty's Ship
Spencer in Cape Cod Bay
September the 30th, 1814

Gentlemen:

It being my intentions to petition as far as lays in my Power the Conduct of the American Forces towards the Defences of Towns in Upper Canada.

I call upon you to come forward with a contribution of One Thousand Dollars for the preservation of your salt works which as I consider of Public Utility will otherwise be destroyed.

I have requested the Selectmen of Eastham to deliver or forward this to you.

The very moderate sum of One Thousand Dollars will I hope cause you to come forward without delay and shall expect on the sixth of October next you will have the above sum ready to deliver on board any one of his Britannick Majesty's Ships belonging to the squadron under my orders that may arrive in the Bay.

On delivery of said sum a Certificate Guaranteeing the safety of the Salt Works of Orleans, during the present war will be given and its safety insured.

Your not complying with the Terms as above will cause me to suppose you Intend defending the said works and I must therefore take steps accordingly.

I am

Gentlemen Your Most
Humble Obedient Servant

Richard Raggot, Captain

His Britannick Majesty's Ship
Spencer Senior Officer in
Boston Bay

To: The Selectmen and Proprietors
of the Salt Works of Orleans.

The Barnstable Patriot, November 30, 1858.

THE SALT MANUFACTURE - The manufacture of salt in this county will soon be abandoned. No new works have been erected during the last quarter of a century, and every year some of the old are broken up. At the present price of salt it cannot be made at a profit, by solar evaporation. The first settlers made salt by boiling sea water, an expensive and tedious process. During the Revolutionary war, salt sold at three dollars a bushel, and the old method was again resorted to of boiling from sea water. At Harwich, Job Chase and Obed E. Smith, had twelve kettles of 16 galls each set in mason works, and a pump to raise the water. They continued the manufacture of salt by boiling about twenty years. There were many other small establishments for making salt, by boiling during the Revolution.

Mr. John Sears was the first to manufacture salt in New England in works constructed on the principle they now are. - He commenced his experiments during the Revolutionary war, but he did not perfect his plan till 1796-7. At first he bailed water with buckets into his works. A little before the close of the Revolution, he procured one of the pumps of the British ship of war *Somerset,* wrecked on the coast, and pumped the water by hand. In 1790 he invented and put in operation a mill for raising water, similar to those now in use. In 1795 at the suggestion of Edward Sears, he placed the covers of his works on rollers, so that they could be moved easily and expeditiously opened and shut.

Mr. John Sears claimed to be the original discoverer of this mode of manufacturing salt, and obtained letters patent of which the following is a copy:

THE UNITED STATES OF AMERICA

To all whom these Letters Patent shall come. Whereas, John Sears, a citizen of the State of Massachusetts, in the United States, hath alleged that he has invented a new and useful improvement, to wit, a machine for the purpose of manufacturing salt from salt water by the operation of the rays of the sun upon the water placed therein: which improvement, has not been known or used before his application - has made oath that he verily believe that he is the true inventor or discoverer of the said improvement, has paid into the Treasury of the United States, the sum of thirty dollars, delivered a receipt for the same and presented a petition to the Secretary of State signifying a desire of obtaining an exclusive property in the said Improvement, and praying that a Patent may be granted for that purpose: These are therefore to grant according to laws to the said John Sears, his heirs, administrators and assigns, for the term of fourteen years from the twenty-fourth day of the present month of January, the full and exclusive right and liberty of making, constructing, using and vending to others to be used, the said improvement, a description whereof is given in the words of said John Sears, himself, in the schedule hereto annexed, and is made a part of these presents.

In testimony whereof I have caused these letters to be made patent and the Seals of the United States to be hereunto affixed. Given under my hand at the City of Philadelphia, this twenty-fourth day of January in the year of our lord one thousand seven hundred and ninety-nine, and of the Independence of the United States of America the twenty-third.

JOHN ADAMS

By the President. TIMOTHY PICKERING, Sec'y of State.

City of Philadelphia, to wit: I do hereby certify that the foregoing Letters Patent were delivered to me on the twenty-second day of January, in the year of our Lord one thousand seven hundred and ninety-nine, to be examined, that I have examined the same and find them conformable to law, and I do hereby return the same to the Secretary of State within fifteen days from the date aforesaid, to wit, on this twenty-second day of January in the year aforesaid.

CHARLES LEE, Attorney General.

[The schedule referred to in the foregoing Letters Patent, gives a description of ordinary salt-works, not materially different from those now in existence, and which it is not necessary to print.]

The vats or troughs were only ten feet wide and the covers of the same width, making when open the twenty feet, named in the description.

In 1802, Mr. Hatsel Kelley of Dennis invented crane salt-works and made many improvements on the Sears invention. He also obtained a patent for his improvements. They joined their interest; but their claims as original inventors was successfully contested in the United States Courts. John Sears, Edward Sears, Christopher and William Crowell, were joint owners of the works described in the aforesaid schedule. It was proved in court by a witness from the Isle of Shoals that William Crowell, one of the partners, had seen and examined a salt-work built at that island before Sears built his, and embracing the same principle. It is too late now to question the decision of the court; but it did not appear very clearly by the testimony of the witness that much if any salt had ever been made at the Isle of Shoals by solar evaporation.

The chemical properties of the bittern were not known to Mr. Sears when he applied for his patent. He afterwards manufactured the Glauber's salt, which he retailed, in Dennis and the adjacent towns. In connection with this manufacture an anecdote is told of the late Doct. Samuel Savage of Barnstable. When the Doct. settled in Barnstable he made much use of Glauber's salt and recommended it as the best of family medicine. He kept it for sale and sold hundreds of portions at 1s 4d each. When John Sears commenced retailing it at 1s 6d per pound, the Doct. sold few portions at 1s 4d. In a few years, there were many manufacturers and the price was reduced to four pence, half penny per pound. One of them offered to sell the Doct. at that price. "No," he said, "they are d... cold things, not fit to give a dog."

The first works were called "John Sears' folly," but those who were foremost in ridiculing his inventions were also foremost in contesting in the courts his claim to the exclusive use of his "Folly." - [Yarmouth Register.]

John Sears obligation to Nathaniel Freeman, November 24, 1798

Know all men by these presents that whereas I, John Sears of Dennis, in the County of Barnstable am instituted to a Patent for erecting Saltworks within the United States, which Patent I am expecting to receive from the Secretary of State at Philadelphia - Now for the consideration of forty dollars, paid me by Nathaniel Freeman of Harwich aforesaid gentleman the receipt whereof I do hereby acknowledge, do hereby give, grant, sell and convey unto him the said Nathaniel Freeman, his heirs and assigns forever, all my right title and interest in and unto said Patent which I now or ever shall have so far as it relates to Saltworks, which now are or shall hereafter be erected or built in the Towns of Harwich, Orleans and Chatham, in the County of Barnstable aforesaid and I do hereby agree, promise and oblige myself, that at anytime after receiving a Patent for erecting or building Saltworks and which Patent I hereby obligate myself _____ or take out I will upon request of said Nathaniel Freeman execute to him, his heirs or assigns a more particular and simple instrument or conveyance of all right and title, which I may have by virtue of any Patent I may have or receive for erecting saltworks, as aforesaid so far as the same shall relate to those saltworks which are or may be erected in the Towns of Harwich, Chatham and Orleans aforesaid. To the true and faithful performance of all the agreements and promises contained in this Instrument, I bind myself, my heirs and assigns unto him the said Nathaniel Freeman, his heirs and assigns in the sum and penalty of two hundred dollars, witness my hand and seal at Harwich aforesaid this 24th day of November AD One Thousand seven hundred Ninety eight.

John Sears, Junior.

Signed sealed and delivered
in the presence of

Henry Sears.

Nathaniel Freeman's obligation to Reuben Ryder, 12 May, 1800.

Know all men by these presents that I, Nathaniel Freeman of Harwich in the County of Barnstable, Agent for and in consideration of Twenty dollars paid me by Reuben Ryder of Chatham in the County aforesaid which I do acknowledge to have recieved, do hereby give, grant and sell unto said Reuben Ryder, his heirs and assigns full liberty to erect Saltworks at his own proper cost and charge within the town of Chatham aforesaid, in any quantity whatsoever. No persons to be interested in the same but himself for the term of fourteen years from the twentyfourth day of January, one thousand seven hundred and ninety nine. That being the date of a patent John Sears of Dennis has obtained for the exclusive right of erecting, using and vending to others to be used, saltworks or a machine for the purpose of making salt from salt water, part of which rights the said John Sears has conveyed to me which includes the Town of Chatham and I do covenant and agree with the said Reuben Ryder, his heirs and assigns, that I will free him from any cost or charge whatsoever, which the aforesaid John Sears by virtue of the aforesaid patent had a right to demand for the use of the aforesaid machine for making salt so far as respects any saltworks which the said Reuben Ryder at his own proper cost and charge shall erect within the limits of the Town of Chatham aforesaid, for the term of fourteen years as aforesaid to the true and faithful performance of this covenant or agreement I bind myself, my heirs and assigns to the said Reuben Ryder, his heirs and assigns in the sum and penalty of One hundred dollars. In witness whereof I have here unto set my hand and seal at Harwich this day of May 12th, Anno Domini One Thousand and eight hundred.

Nathaniel Freeman

In presence of

Silvanus Stone
Anthony Gray.

Observations upon the art of extracting Marine Salt from sea water, by evaporation, produced by the sun's heat; with a description of the works, and the several processes used in preparing Medicinal Salts, and Magnesia Alba.

By: James Thacher, M.D., F.A.A.

Historical Society of Old Yarmouth, Yarmouthport, Massachusetts
Historic Research Funds, February 1975.

Every essay having in view the advancement of our manufactures, and encouraging the efforts of industry, will, it is presumed, receive the approbation of every class and description of society. From this source, results that substantial advantage, to realize which, the public has an undoubted claim upon the energy and exertions of individual citizens. An enterprise, which associates private emolument with general interest, may with peculiar propriety be recommended to the consideration of the community.

While then the active labourer is employed in exploring the bowels of the earth for riches, while the adventurous seaman hazards his safety upon the stormy billows, traversing the mighty deep in pursuit of treasure, shall we not reach forth our hands to receive that bounty of providence, which constantly flows at our shores, and daily washes the borders of our farms?

These preliminary remarks have reference to the art of extracting common salt from sea water by evaporation, which till within a short period was unknown among the inhabitants of this country, and even at this time a knowledge of the business is confined almost exclusively to the shores of Cape Cod.

A want of particular information respecting this productive branch of manufacture, has hitherto prevented its being more extensively beneficial. An apology therefore for this communication, were it not for its imperfections, would be unnecessary. Let it however be observed, that in endeavouring to assist the uninformed artist, I am not solicitous to vie with those who are in pursuit of literary fame.

The method of preparing and refining salt in the salterns in different parts of Europe, would not comport with the circumstances of our country. The superior advantages of our procedure consists in dissipating the water without the expense of fuel, the furnace and other apparatus for boiling. "The fuel alone expended in some of their salterns, costs more than two thirds the value of the salt." Omitting therefore any particular detail respecting the processes used in the preparation of salt in other parts of the world, the subsequent observations will relate entirely to the successful experiments, which commenced with, and are now prosecuted by the industrious inhabitants of Cape Cod.

During the distressful period of our Revolutionary War, Mr. John Sears, with two or three associates, were the first who commenced at Dennis the manufacture of salt by evaporation; their unpromising attempts were deemed chimerical; but by a commendable perseverance, they repelled the obloquy of the incredulous, and in due season realized a profit exceeding their most sanguine expectations.

The undertaking has since been greatly improved, and become an establishment meriting public consideration, and as respects the peculiar circumstances of the inhabitants upon the Cape, may be viewed as an acquisition of inestimable value.

The works now erected in the county of Barnstable, from their advantageous situation and extent, are calculated to produce annually an immense quantity both of marine and glauber salt; the particular amount cannot at present be ascertained. One man in the town of Yarmouth, has upon his farm a valuable set of works, consisting of 130,000 superficial feet; the annual produce of which he estimates at upwards of 520 hogsheads of marine, besides a due proportion of glauber salt, amounting to about nine tons. This gentleman, with many others, are now augmenting their works in the confident expectation of realizing a clear profit from 25 to 35 per cent. Some works possessing peculiar advantage in point of situation, have yielded a greater profit; and proprietors in general calculate upon defraying the expense of their works in four or five years. The average produce, is for every 1,000 superficial feet, 33 bushels of marine, and 150 pounds glauber salts. The quality of the salt is equal to any imported. It weighs 80 pounds per bushel, and is decidedly superior in point of strength to foreign salt, if in this respect we except that which is made during the extreme heat of July and August, which in consequence of a hasty evaporation, retains a portion of the bittern. This weakens the salt, makes it more soluble, and less proper for domestic use than that manufactured in the more temperate months. Liverpool salt is so strongly impregnated with lime, that fish cured with it have the appearance of being *whitewashed,* which greatly injures their market.* Our works are remarkably well adapted to free the salt from this and other impurities; and it is from the separation of this substance, that our salt acquires its peculiar whiteness and purity.

Considering the duty imposed on foreign salt, the freight and charges of that bulky commodity, our manufacturies can even in time of peace afford to undersell our importers.

When, therefore, our enterprise shall have progressed to that desirable extent to which the importance of the object, and the success of our experiments encourage us to hope, we may exhibit upon our shores a source of wealth little inferior to the celebrated salt mine of Cracow.**

John Sears and Hallet Kelly, late of Dennis, have both obtained patents for their different plans of constructing the works, which are held in competition, nor has experience satisfactorily decided, which possesses the

* For some of these particulars, I am indebted to the information and intelligence of the Reverend Mr. Briggs of Chatham.

** Some of the salt mines are of amazing magnitude, the single mine of Cracow in Poland, is computed to hold salt enough to supply the whole world for many thousand years. There are houses, chapels, &c. under ground all built of salt, or the salt stones. The fossil is cut and turned into pillars, altars, crucifixes, images, &c. Often times it is naturally crystallized into very curious figures. Masses are sometimes brought up weighing from 20 to 30 cwt. *Neumann's Chem. Vol. I, Page 330.*

strongest claim to preference.* Their respective advantages, however, will appear from the particular description which follows.

In the first place a commodious situation near the shore should be made choice of, where the rays of the sun can fall with the greatest possible effect; and to render this more efficient, the vats should be built in a line extending from east to west. Conformably to Sears' plan, a vat 16 feet wide is to be erected on stands of cedar rails or other small timber, at a convenient height from the ground, care being taken to place a double board under every stand to prevent their settling. The frame is commonly formed of pine, hemlock or other joist. The largest or side timbers being 4 by 5 inches, and the middle ones 3 by 4. The floor is made of good seasoned boards nailed upon this frame. A piece of plank, about six inches in width, is placed upon its edge on top of the outside timber, resting upon the ends of the floor boards, and firmly secured by upright pieces, trundled on the outside, at proper distances from each other, in the form of dovetail; but an improvement in this method is, that the gunwale plank should supply the place of the side timber, having a groove within one inch of its lower edge, into which the ends of the floor boards are inserted. This building must be divided by plank partitions into three apartments; the water room being the largest, must occupy two thirds of the whole; the pickle room takes up two thirds of the remainder, and the residue is assigned for the salt room.

The two last rooms must fall each a few inches below the one immediately preceding, for the convenience of drawing off the liquor.

It is a point of importance, that the floor of the salt room in particular, be perfectly tight; to this end, none but the best of seasoned boards, planed on one side, and entirely clear of sap, and loose knots should be used. The joints, especially under the gunwale, should be caulked and payed. The covers or roofs should be made as light as possible; they must, however, effectually secure the vats from rain, as that would greatly injure

* Sears' patent is contested upon the principle of his not being the original inventor, which question is now pending before the Circuit Court for decision.

the process, by diluting the pickle, and impeding the evaporation. They are in the form of the common pitched roof with gable ends. They should be ten feet in width, so that a vat one hundred feet long, will require ten covers. The two pieces of cross joist, which support the roofs, are furnished with shivers, or small wheels of cast iron, or hard wood, and also side shivers, placed horizontally, to accelerate their motion. Small strips of plank should be extended from the vats, supported by proper stands, for the purpose of rolling off the covers. The roofs have usually been covered with ordinary boards, except those over the salt room, which we are advised to shingle; but a better method unquestionably is, instead of boards, to cover the frames with shingles nailed upon small rafters. In either case I would urge the expediency of painting the roofs white, for the double purpose of preserving the wood, and its power of increasing the reflection of solar heat.

The invention of the late Hallet Kelly, comes next under consideration; he directs the vats to be made in the form of a parallelogram, 20 by 40 feet; two of these join together at their angles, and communicate by a spout. At the angular point is erected a perpendicular post of proper height, upon the top of which is balanced a large cross beam, firmly braced; the covers upon this plan have hipped roofs, are twenty feet square, being a pair to each vat, and suspended one at each end of this beam; may be compared to a pair of brass scales inverted with their beam placed upon a fulcrum. The post is furnished with a pivot at the bottom, turns off in the manner of a crane, and covers then occupy the interval between the two vats. Thus a line of works may be erected of an indefinite length in zig zag form, with a crane post standing alternately between every vat, and the whole to be connected by spouts.

It will at first view be perceived, that this piece of machinery is calculated to turn with great ease and celerity, and it is conceded that a greater extent of works can be covered and uncovered in a given time upon this, than the former plan; but it is objected by the advocates of Sear's method, that the suspended weight will derange the post and repairs become frequently requisite; that they do not so effectually secure the vats from rain, and that they occupy more ground than the others. Some gentlemen, however, in whose hands both methods have passed the test of experience, assure me, that Kelly's invention deserves the preference, although the difference in the cost is estimated at 7 per cent. In fact the works upon either plan are completely under control, and require very little manual aid to cover them, when rain is expected.

Contiguous to the vats, it is necessary to erect a mill and pump for every 20,000 superficial feet of works, to complete the apparatus. The pump is placed in a small cistern, sunk to the level of the tide water, from which is carried a subterraneous pipe, towards low water mark. A small windmill, with canvas sails, being now connected with the pump, the water is thrown into spouts, and conveyed to every part of the works, as occasion may require. Having now completed the machinery, and brought the proprietor to that stage of the business in which he may anticipate his compensation; it is next incumbent upon me to describe particularly the process, by which the different kinds of salt are usually obtained. In doing this, I shall have regard to the order in which the occurrences will successively result.

The water being pumped into the water room, immediately after being finished, that the work may swell and become tight, should continue there until a considerable part if it has evaporated, and the residue acquired the strength and sharpness of brine. The plugs are then to be withdrawn from the partition, and the liquor let into the pickle room. The length of time required for its continuance in the first room, must evidently depend upon the degree of heat to which it has been exposed; but for the precise time of drawing the liquor out of the pickle room, we have a more correct criterion; for in this stage of the process, a calcareous earth of lime begins to appear upon the surface, and soon subsides to the bottom in the form of a white earthy powder. Soon after this occurrence, the liquor being almost fully saturated with salt, exhibits a saline pellicle upon its surface; and in a dry day small crystals begin to form, which immediately concrete into corns, resembling hail, and precipitate to the bottom. The subsidence of the lime, therefore, and the appearance of granulated salt, mark the point of time, when the pickle should be drawn into the salt room. In this last stage of the process, the liquor from further evaporation becomes highly concentrated, and the salt, accumulating upon the floor, assumes its natural crystalline form.

The salt should remain in the salt room, till a large quantity is procured, and more pickle added to it occasionally. When removed into the store house, should be placed upon a shelving floor, that the saline liquor may be entirely drained from it.

The next subject that should arrest our attention, is the preparation of the two kinds of medicinal salt procured at the works. The first is obtained in the form of large beautiful crystals, scarcely distinguishable from the genuine sal mirabile, or glauber salt, and is found to be equal in quality to the best imported salts used in medicine. The manufacture of this valuable article is progressing to such extent and perfection, as to meet the demand of the United States, and render importation altogether unnecessary. It has also become an article of some consequence in commerce. Many tons of it are annually exported to the East and West Indies, where I learn it comes to a ready and profitable market. Some objections have been made to this salt, on account of the large size of its crystals; but this circumstance does not affect it medicinal virtues, and its repute in medicine has the sanction of experience.

This salt is procured during the cold weather in winter, from the pickle or brine in its concentrated state, and the same result will ensue, whether we have recourse to the process antecedent or subsequent to the crystallization of the sea salt. Having procured a quantity of pickle, sufficiently inspissated in the salt, it is to be exposed to the cold weather in the vats during the winter, from the effects of which the salt will be found to shoot into irregular crystals, and precipitate to the bottom. In order to purify this salt; it must be taken out, put into a copper boiler, being first half filled with warm fresh water; with which the salt it to be dissolved and boiled for some time. The solution, after standing an hour or two in a wooden vessel for the faeces to subside, should be poured off from the sediment into coolers, where the salt will immediately form into perfect crystals; should the salt not be quite pure, nor assume the form of regular crystals, it may be redissolved, and the operation repeated. After the crystallization of both marine salt and sal glauber, there remains upon the floor of the salt room a saline bitter liquor, called mother, lye or bittern. This liquor has commonly been thrown away as useless; but the workmen should be apprised that it will yield both a neutral salt and magnesia alba. If this bittern be set by in a cold place for sometime in a leaden vessel, a quantity of glauber salt, before mentioned, will shoot; and if the remainder of the bittern be gently evaporated farther, a fresh quantity of the same kind of salt will appear; but if the bittern be hastily evaporated by boiling, and set to cool, salt will be produced in the form of fine delicate needle point crystals; having, when taken out of the liquid, the appearance of snow. This is no other than the genuine bitter cathartic salt of Epsom, so called from the mineral spring of Epsom, where it was originally discovered by Dr. Grew. Although this and the glauber salt are in their chemical properties essentially dissimilar, they are in medicinal virtues nearly allied, and often prescribed indiscriminately. Another article in the preparation of which some attempts have been made at the works on the Cape, is magnesia alba. The specimens of it, which I have inspected, are manifestly inferior to English magnesia. "That prepared directly from the bittern, is by no means equal in purity to that produced from Epsom salt."

Our workmen are confusedly unacquainted with the most eligible method of obtaining it in genuine purity; nor can they have accurate idea's upon the subject unless they possess some knowledge of the laws of chemical affinity, and the powers of elective attraction. Incidents influenced by these principles, although perfectly familiar to the mind of every chemical operator, would be considered by those not versed in that science, as inexplicable phenomena. Referring to chemical writers for further information, it will suffice for our purpose to observe, than an acid and alkali possess opposite principles, and that a combination of the two, form a neutral compound. Epsom salts is precisely in this predicament, being formed by a combination of an absorbent earth, or magnesia and the vitriolic acid. It is by the decomposition of Epsom salt, or disunion of these constituent parts, that we obtain genuine magnesia. There is a diversity in the minutia of the process even in the hands of chemical operators; but since Mr. Henry, of Manchester, (England) has improved upon the process, and his magnesia having justly obtained celebrity and preference on account of its delicate whiteness and purity, his method should be recommended as most eligible for our imitation. The following is not essentially varient from Mr. Henry's process. "Take any quantity of Epsom salt, dissolve it in boiling water, and filter the solution. Dissolve also half the quantity of good pearl ash, and filter the solution. Both of these solutions ought to be somewhat diluted, and it will be proper to use twice the quantity of water, which would fairly dissolve the salts. Mix the two solutions when nearly cold, and stir them very well together. Let the mixture stand for some hours, until the precipitate has fallen to the bottom in form of a coarse gritty powder. Put the whole then into a clean copper kettle, under which a moderate fire is made. Stir the matter incessantly with a large wooden spatula, to prevent the powder from sticking to the bottom. As the mixture heats, the powder begins to loose its sandy appearance, and to increase greatly in quantity; so that though at first the mixture was quite thin, with only a small portion of sandy matter amongst it, before it has attained the boiling heat, it will be so thick that it can scarcely be stirred. When the grittiness is quite gone, the matter must be put upon a filtering cloth, and warm water poured upon it, till it runs insipid. The magnesia is then to be put upon chalk stones, which will absorb the greatest part of the moisture, and it may at last be fully dried in a stove."*

In preparing this medicine, no point in the process is more important, than the repeated ablutions with soft pure water. The hardness of that from some wells and springs, renders it altogether improper for the purpose; but soft river or rain water, after being filtrated through a thick linen cloth, will answer equally as well as distilled water, recommended by some operators. The ablutions, however, should be repeated until the medicine be reduced to an impalpable powder, free from all grittiness or

* See Encyclopedia, Motherby's Medical Dictionary, and Quincy's Dispensatory, 15th edition, Appendix.

other impurities. The chalk stones employed for the purpose of drying, should be frequently cleaned and exposed to a moderate degree of heat, and the powder enclosed in sheets of white paper, and carefully dried before the fire or in a furnace.

Thus have I endeavoured to contribute my mite to the common interest; and however deficient my claim to general applause, I can repose with confidence in the hope of *candor* from the patrons of the Arts and Sciences.

Such is the interesting nature of this subject, that the propriety of a communication to the Academy of Arts and Sciences has been suggested, and should it afford satisfaction to that learned and respectable Association, and in any measure aid the spirit of industry and enterprise in our country, I shall realize an ample reward.

I have the honor to subscribe myself, Gentlemen, with sentiments of profound respect, your most obedient, humble servant,

JAMES THACHER.

Plymouth, August 16th, 1802.

Appendix

HOUSE....No. 31.

COMMONWEALTH OF MASSACHUSETTS.

In the House of Representatives, Jan. 4, 1840. - Ordered, That a Committee of five be appointed, with such as the Senate may join, to take into consideration and report upon the expediency of instructing our Senators, and requesting our Representatives in Congress, to oppose the passage of a bill introduced into the Senate of the United States, December 27, 1839, for repealing the act laying a duty upon imported salt, granting a bounty upon pickled fish exported, and allowing bounty to vessels employed in the fisheries: and the following gentlemen are appointed to constitute the Committee, namely:

> Messrs. Loring of *Hingham,*
> Russell, of *Plymouth,*
> Parrot, of *Boston,*
> Jones, of *Falmouth,*
> and Lewis, of *Barnstable.*

> Sent up for concurrence,

> L.S. Cushing, *Clerk.*

In Senate, Jan. 5, 1840.

Concurred, and Messrs. Sprague, Hooper, Lane and Marston, are joined.

> Cha's Calhoun, *Clerk.*

The joint special Committee, to whom was referred an order directing them to consider and report upon the expediency of instructing our senators, and requesting our representatives, in Congress, to oppose the passage of a bill introduced into the senate of the United States, December 27, 1839, for repealing the act laying a duty upon imported salt, and granting a bounty upon pickled fish exported, and allowing a bounty to vessels employed in the fisheries, have attended to the subject and ask leave respectfully to REPORT,

That this subject, having been acted upon by the Legislature the last year, we much regret that there should be occasion to reiterate our objections to a repeal of the duty on salt, and the bounty to the vessels and men employed in the cod-fishery, as provided by a bill introduced into the senate of the United States, at their present session. Was this measure to affect some local interest - to cut off the means by which a small portion of our citizens obtained their bread, we might not have thought it necessary to enter a formal protest against it. However painful it may be to witness the destruction of capital, or to see our citizens deprived of the means of support, there are no sacrifices we are not ready to make, which the honor or interest of our common country may demand. But we cannot view the measure proposed, as called for by the best interests of any portion of our country. We had consoled ourselves with the thought, that our citizens could rely on the action which Congress has heretofore had on subjects connected with the manufacturing interests of the country, for a few years to come at least; and that our domestic tranquillity was not to be disturbed by incessant changes of policy.

The manufacture of salt in this Commonwealth, is thought to be on the decline, - present prices not being sufficient to induce new investments of capital. The further reduction of duty which is yet to take place, and the apprehension of a further decline in price, has induced many to neglect their works, and where extensive repairs have been deemed necessary, to break them up. It may confidently be predicted, that any measure effecting a further decline in prices, will in a few years, insure the entire destruction of the whole; and thus occasion the loss of an outlay of not less than two millions of dollars, and an annual product, of not less than eight hundred thousand bushels of salt.

The benefits resulting from a home supply in time of war, will, alone, more than counterbalance a duty of six cents a bushel, in time of peace.

The committee doubt the correctness of an opinion prevailing with some persons, that the price of salt will diminish in a corresponding ratio with the duty. In some instances where dutied articles have been admitted free, prices have advanced in the foreign market, and instead of benefiting the consumer, the foreign laborer and manufacturer have reaped the advantage.

In the absence of home manufacture, the article would be of unsteady and unequal supply, and would more easily be monopolized by speculators, and thus the price enhanced to the consumer.

The people of this Commonwealth can never believe it sound policy to employ foreign nations to manufacture articles which they have the means of producing - they cannot believe it can benefit the nation to pay our *silver* and *gold* to make foreign laborers rich, at the expense of her own working men. But, however desirable it may be, to secure in time of war, a supply of an article necessary to health, comfort, and existence, and to give employment to home industry, or to save from destruction a large amount of capital, still, the committee cannot but deem the salt manufacture of little importance, when compared with that of our bank and other cod fisheries.

There are considerations connected with the cod fishery which are of vital importance, and claim the attention of the national Legislature.

The first Congress held under the Constitution, granted a bounty to the fishing industry of the country. The fisheries were subject to the investigation and deliberation of the national Legislature, for many successive years. The numerous reports on the subject, have all borne testimony to their great importance; not particularly regarding the persons immediately engaged in them, or the section of the country in which they are carried on, or the commodity itself as furnishing a wholesome and cheap article for human subsistence; but considering them as affording the best, and surest means, of raising up a class of men, not only useful, but actually necessary to our commerce and navigation, and especially to our naval defence.

All nationals having a naval force, have viewed the fisheries as a nursery for the best and most skillful seamen; and we have only to look at the history of past European conflicts, to see the superior advantages of good seamen in naval warfare. Mr. Jefferson, in a report made to the House of Representatives, when Secretary of State, says, "this rapid view of the cod fishery enables us to discern under what policy it has flourished or declined, in the hands of other nations, and to mark the fact, that it is too poor a business to be left to itself, even with the nation most favorably situated." Subsequent reports have held the same language, both as to the unprofitableness of the business, and its importance to our national marine. To make first-rate seamen, they must be trained to the seas in early life. Most of our fishermen commence at a very early age, frequently at ten or twelve years; a new stock is constantly coming forward to supply the place of those who take to the merchant or naval service.

That other objects have been kept in view, than the mere drawback for the duty on salt, is evident from the fact that the bounty has not been graduated by the duty.

That Great Britain views her cod fishery of great national importance, we may safely infer from the liberal grants and privileges secured to them.

Those who carry on our cod fishery are not rich, but generally in very moderate circumstances. Frequently a single vessel, the value of which does not exceed two or three thousand dollars, has several owners, and those who spend their lives on the fishing banks, are men who, from their earliest years, have been enured to toil and hardships, accustomed to dangers and perils, and are thus eminently fitted for their country's service in time of war. If scientific officers are necessary to our army, and it be of sufficient importance to engage the attention of Congress, surely a supply of seamen for our navy demands their serious and constant attention. If the treasury can be taxed to educate officers for such a purpose, we cannot think the small sums paid to our fishermen are misapplied.

Great martial enterprises may be accomplished without science, but not without physical strength and courage. Our fisheries are of vastly greater importance to the navy, than the West Point Academy is to the army. If the latter furnish science and skill to direct, the former furnishes bone and muscle to accomplish.

The propriety of granting a bounty to our fishermen, having been established upon a principle peculiar to itself, at a time when we were free from sectional jealousies and party spirit, cannot now be called in question, or furnish a precedent for other objects.

That Congress have been desirous of increasing the number of American seamen, is evident from the law requiring the officers and two thirds of the crews of our merchant-ships to be Americans. It is with some difficulty that this law is complied with, as a large proportion of our seamen are not only of foreign origin, but continue to be aliens, some of them have some evidence of citizenship, but doubts may be justly entertained whether they really are such.

The number of native American seamen by no means keeps pace with our increase of population, our commerce, or out national wants. That our national ships should be manned with men, not only of foreign origin, but men whose habits of thinking and acting are inconsistent with the institutions of our country - men who have no wives or children to fight for - whose home is the wide world - and who lose or gain little by a change of masters - must be a matter of serious concern to every friend to his country. Any measure which diminishes the number of native American seamen, affects us in a part vital to our honor, and influence among the nations of the earth. Our fishermen are native Americans, they have no security in the shape of wages, they go on shares, furnishing their own food and other outfits. In case of failure of success in taking fish, (which happens to many every season,) they return with a debt which they are unable to discharge, and destitute of the means of supporting their families during the ensuing winter. In such cases the bounty comes opportunely to save them from want and distress. Should the bill now before Congress become a law, our fisheries must suffer great diminution, and in many places be totally ruined.

The natural advantages enjoyed by the British colonies in America, with the bounty and privileges secured to them, enable them to undersell us in nearly all foreign markets; and should the encouragement heretofore given to our fishermen be withdrawn, there is reason to apprehend they will, to a considerable extent, supply even our own domestic consumption. Our national honor and security ought not to be weighed in the balance with dollars and cents. We ask for no special favors. But we earnestly insist, that justice to those engaged in this laborious and humble occupation, requires that the protection under which they have devoted themselves to it, should not be withdrawn; and that the honor and security of our common country are deeply involved in the continuance of a policy which has been found ever since the organization of the government, essential to the production of American seamen, for the manning of our navy.

But should Congress otherwise determine, we must console ourselves with the ability the people of this Commonwealth possess, of accommodating themselves to their condition, and by the force of their industry, enterprise, and untiring perseverance, provide against adverse circumstances, and bring to their aid resources hitherto unavailing.

In accordance with these views, we recommend the following resolves.

SETH SPRAGUE, Jr., SAMUEL LANE, CHARLES MARSTON, THOMAS LORING, WM. W. PARROTT, THOMAS B. LEWIS, SILAS JONES.

RESOLVES

Concerning the Duty on Salt, and the Bounty to Fishing Vessels.

Resolved, That the repeal of the duty on salt, and the bounty to fishing vessels and the men employed in them, would injuriously affect the best interests of the American people - distress a large portion of our most valuable and deserving citizens - impair our national strength, and weaken us in a part most vital to our honor, and influence, among the nations of the earth.

Resolved, That the passage of the bill now before the senate of the United States, must destroy our salt manufactories, paralyze our cod fisheries, and show that the best interests of the nation will be sacrificed, only to retard our prosperity, and to check the progress of northern industry.

Resolved, That his Excellency the Governor, be requested to transmit copies of these resolves to the senators and representatives of this Commonwealth in Congress.

ACKNOWLEDGMENTS

The collection of photographs and assembly of information for this book was made possible by a large number of people. Many have helped me with the research and development. One of the primary contributors was David Schofield of Orleans. Dave assisted me in the interpretation and collection of several early maps which appear throughout the book. In addition to those listed in the credit lines of the photos there are many others who helped me with accurate information and made contributions to the book. They are: Charlotte Price, Librarian of the Nickerson Room at Cape Cod Community College, Mr. & Mrs. David Sears of East Dennis, Susan Klein and Lexa Crane at Stugis Library in Barnstable, Alec and Audrey Todd of Yarmouth, Robert Farson, Louis Cataldo, Noel Beyle, John Ullman, Rowena Myers, Benjamin Muse, Gordon Caldwell, Frank Ackerman, Lynn Horton, Barry Homer, John Fish, and my artist-historian friend Paul C. Morris of Nantucket. I wish to thank the personnel of the several Libraries and Historical Societies listed below for allowing me access to their collections. The information gleaned from these sources enabled me to fit the many pieces of this puzzle together. A final thought for my late brother Howard, who encouraged me to go ahead with the work of assembling and finishing the manuscript.

W.P.Q.

Libraries: St. Petersburg, Florida Public Library, Boston Public Library, New Bedford Public Library, Sturgis Library in Barnstable, Yarmouth Library, Jacob Sears Memorial Library in East Dennis, Provincetown Library and Snow Library, Orleans.

Museums & Historical Societies: Dennis Historical Society, Brewster Historical Society, Orleans Historical Society, Massachusetts State House Archives and Sandwich Glass Museum.

Bibliography

Bailey, Thomas A., *The American Pageant-History of the Republic* - 1971

Baker, Florence W., *Yesterday's Tide* - 1941

Barber, John Warner, *Historical Collections of Massachusetts* - 1840

Barber, Laurence, *When South Yarmouth was Quaker Village* - 1988

Barnstable County, *Three Centuries of the Cape Cod County* - 1985

Barnstable, Town of, *The Seven Villages of Barnstable* - 1976

Boston Chamber of Commerce, *New England*, Edited by George French - 1911

Brigham, Albert Perry, *Cape Cod and the Old Colony* - 1921

Commonwealth of Massachusetts, *The Population and Resources of Cape Cod* - 1922

_____ *The Historical and Archaeological Resources of Cape Cod and the Islands* - 1987

_____ *Massachusetts Business Directory* - 1835

_____ *Massachusetts Register for the year* 1859

_____ *Revised Statutes for the year 1835*

_____ *State Record & Year Book of General Information* - 1850

_____ *Statistics, Industry, Massachusetts* - 1845

Deyo, Simeon L., *History of Barnstable County* - 1890

Digges, Jeremiah, *Cape Cod Pilot* - 1937

Doane, Alfred A., *The Doane Family Genealogy* - 1960

Drake, S.A., *Nooks and Corners of the New England Coast* - 1875

Earle, Alice Morse, *Stage Coach and Tavern Days* - 1900

Fairburn, Wm. Armstrong, *Merchant Sail*, Volume I - 1947

Falmouth Historical Comm., *The Book of Falmouth* - 1986

Fawsett, Marise, *Cape Cod Annals* - 1990

Freeman, Frederick, *History of Cape Cod* - 1858

Geoffrey, Theodate, *Suckanesset, A History of Falmouth* - 1928

Hufbauer, Virginia Knowles, *Descendants of Richard Knowles* - 1974

Jenkins, E. Lawrence, *Old Quaker Village* - 1915

Kimball, Edward Augustus, *Travels Through Northern U.S.* - 1808

Kittredge, George Lyman, *The Old Farmer and His Almanack* - 1920

Kittredge, Henry C., *Cape Cod, Its People and Their History* - 1930
_____ *Shipmasters of Cape Cod* - 1935
Lossing, Benson J., *Pictorial Field-Book of the War of 1812* - 1868
Lovell, Russell A., Jr, *Sandwich, A Cape Cod Town* - 1984
Mahoney, Haynes R., *Yarmouth's Proud Packets* - 1986
Massachusetts Historical Society, *Collections, Volume VIII* - 1802
May, Samuel P., *Sears Genealogy* - 1890
Morrison, Samuel Eliot, *Maritime History of Massachusetts* - 1921
Nason, Rev. Elias, *Massachusetts Gazetteer* - 1874
Perley, Sidney, *Historic Storms of New England* - 1891
Perry, E.G., *A Trip around Cape Cod* - 1898
Pratt, Rev. Enoch, *History of Eastham, Wellfleet and Orleans* - 1844
Rich, Shebnah, *Truro, Cape Cod* - 1884
Ryder, Alice Austin, *Lands of Sippican* - 1934
Shay, Edith & Frank, *Sand in Their Shoes, A Cape Cod Reader* - 1951
Smith, Nancy Paine, *The Provincetown Book* - 1922
Smith, William C., *A History of Chatham* - 1971
Swift, Charles F., *Cape Cod* - 1897
Swift, C.W., *Cape Cod History & Genealogy* - 1927
Thompson, Elroy S., *History of Plymouth, Norfolk and Barnstable Counties*
Chapter XLI - 1928
Thoreau, Henry, *Cape Cod* - 1865
Trayser, Donald G., *Barnstable, Three Centuries of a Cape Cod Town* - 1939
_____, *Cape Cod Historical Almanac* - 1989
Vuilleumier, Marion, *The Town of Yarmouth, Massachusetts* - 1989
Wood, Donald, *Cape Cod, A Guide* - 1973

Newspapers:

Barnstable Patriot, Hyannis, Mass. - 1830 - 1869
Yarmouth Register, Yarmouth, Mass. - 1836 - 1889

Magazines:

Cape Cod Magazine - 1915, 1916.
American History Illustrated, Year Without a Summer - 1970

Acorn, 85
Adams, John Quincy, 77
American, 7, 8, 27,
Aptuxet Trading Post, 30
Atlantic, 23,
Asia, 38
Australia, 38

Bacon, Ebenezer, 63
Baker, Lorenzo Dow, 199
Barber, John Warner, 171
Barnstable, 50, 55, 59, 73, 105, 113
Barnstable County, v, 26, 42, 45, 55,
    94, 105, 113, 179
Barnstable Patriot, 94, 185, 186, 187,
    189, 191
Bass River, 119, 190
Baxter Mill, 83
Belgium, 50
Belle of the West, 93
Benjamin Franklin, 41
Billingsgate Island, 59
Boston and Sandwich Glass Company,
    85, 87
Boston, 27, 37, 41, 45, 65, 71, 93,
    199, 201
Boston Light, 69
Bourne, 30, 51, 105
Bradford, Governor, 6
Brewster, 38, 47, 52, 55, 63, 73, 83,
    141
Bristol County, 45, 61
British, 7, 27, 45, 47
Brown, Captain William, 59
Brutus, 59
Buzzards Bay, 51, 105

Canadian maritimes, 37,
Cape Ann, 6
Caribbean, 7, 27,
Carolinas, 37,
Chancellor Livingston, 41
Chapman, Lottie, 19
Charles, 107

Chase, Captain Henry B., 114
Chatham, 30, 55, 59, 61, 73, 105, 155
China, 38
Christopher Hall, 93
Civil War, 94, 192, 197
Cobb, Elijah, 63, 188
Collins, Edward Knight, 199
Comet, 114
Concord Coach, 71
Congress, 8
Connecticut, 38, 52
Constitution, 27,
Cook, Captain James, 59
Cook, Captain Samuel, 59
Crocker, John, 50, 107
Crocker, Loring, 47, 113, 188, 189
Crosswell, Samuel P., 63
Crowell, Captain Christopher, 19, 22
Crowell, Captain Levi, 12
Crowell, Captain William, 19, 22

Davis, Senator John, 183, 185
Dennis, 1, 38, 57, 71, 73, 93, 105
Dexter, Thomas, 83
Deyo, Simeon, 23
Drake, Edwin L., 193
Dukes County, 61, 63

East Dennis, 15
Eastham, 26, 52, 55, 59, 73, 83, 105,
    163, 203
East Mill, 77
Ellen Sears, 93
England, v, 6, 45, 47, 50
Erie Canal, 187
Europe, 7, 55, 203

Fall River, 179
Falmouth, 37, 50, 63, 73, 87, 105, 107
Federal Government, 59
Fisher, Charles, 203
Flavilla, 109
Florida, 197

France, 45, 203
Freeman, Captain Samuel, Jr., 63
Freeman, Major Nathaniel, 17
Fulton, Robert, 71

Georges Banks, 57
Globe, 109
Grand Banks, 27,

Hannah, Atty. Samuel D., 31,
Harwich, 17, 55, 73, 105, 141
Henry Clay, 109
Heritage Plantation, 77
Highland Light, 59
Hippogriffe, 93
Holland, 77

Independence, 109
Indians, 6, 8, 32, 33,

Jarves, Deming, 85, 87, 107
Jefferson, President, 45
Jenkins, Capt. Weston, 50, 107
Jernegan, Rev. Prescott, 203
Jones, Silas, 107
J.W. Barber, 8

Kelley, Hattil, 17
Kenney, John, 63
Kimball, Edward A., 35,
Kit Carson, 93
Knowles Connection, 96

Lakin, Josephine Robinson, 19
Longfellow, 174

Mail, 71
Maine, 51
Marstons Mills, 87
Martha's Vineyard, 45
Martinique, 179
Mashpee, 105, 109
Massachusetts, 45, 51, 52, 62, 107,
    197, 199, 201
Massachusetts General Court, 27, 61, 183
Mattacheese, 119

McKay, Donald, 93
Melrose, 174, 176
Minot's Ledge Light, 69
Monomoy, 59, 181
Monomoy Point, 59
Monroe, President James, 77

Namskaket, 145
Nantucket, 45, 73, 80, 179
Nauset, 105
New Bedford, 38, 179
Newcastle, H.M.S., 47
New England, 6, 7, 80, 179, 193, 197,
    201, 203
Newfoundland, 203
New Hampshire, 51
New Jersey, 85
New York, 37, 38
New York City, 179, 181
Nimrod, Brig, 50
Nobska Point, 59
Nobscusset Point Pier, 38,
Norton, Capt. Presbury, 63

Orleans, 9, 41, 55, 73, 83, 105,
    145, 203

Peaked Hill Bars, 17, 59
Peerless, 109
Pilgrims, 6, 33,
Pizarro, 109
Pleasant Bay, 141
Plymouth, 6, 32
Polly, 85, 107
Postboy, 67
Point Allerton, 69
President, 41
Proprietors, 31, 32,
Proprietary Corporations, 31,
Provincetown, 35, 41, 52, 55, 59, 73,
    105, 171, 174, 183, 201

Queen Elizabeth, 47
Quivet Neck, 1, 23, 93

Race Point, 9, 59
Raggett, Captain, Richard, 47, 50, 208
Revenue, 93
Revolutionary War, v, 2, 19, 27, 35,
Rhode Island, 52
Rich, Shebnah, 38, 190
Rock Harbor, 47
Roman Army, 6
Round Cove, 141
Royal Navy, 27,
Ryder, Wm. Smith, Jr., 13

St. Pierre-Miquelon, 203
Sandwich, 107
Sandwich, 41, 51, 55, 73, 85, 87, 105
Sandwich Glass Museum, 85, 87
Sanford, Ephraim, 107
Sappho, 109
Science, 109
Sears, Captain John, 15, 17, 22, 23,
          41, 134
Sears Edward, 19, 22
Sears, Phebe, 15
Sears, Reuben, 17
Sears, Richard, 15
Sesuit, 23, 93
Shiverick, Asa, 93
South America, 38,
South Yarmouth, 27,
Sparrowhawk, 145
Spencer, H.M.S., 47
Splendid, 107
Star, 93
Sturgis Library, 189
Swift, Elijah, 107
Swift, C.W., 31,

T-Wharf, 69
Temperance, 109
Thacher, James, 30,
Thoreau, Henry David, 27, 41, 42, 80,
          94, 183
Truro, 35, 55, 57, 59, 73, 105, 168,
          190, 199
Tudor, Fredric, 179

Ulysses, 59
United States, 55, 197
U.S. Congress, 50

Vermont, 51
Volant, 109
Volusia, 59

War of 1812, 45, 52
Washington, 41
Webfoot, 93
Wellfleet, 38, 55, 59, 73, 105, 167, 190
West Indies, 27, 38, 55
Wild Hunter, 93
Wirt, William, 77
Woods Hole, 59

Yarmouth, 1, 12, 55, 73, 105, 119,
          187, 190
Yarmouth Register, 85
Young, Capt. A.H., 71

Akin, Abiel, 119
Akin, David, 119
Ames, Thomas, 113
Arey, Joseph, 146
Arey, Thomas, 146
Armstrong, Edward, 168
Atkins, Freeman, 168
Atkins, Joshua, 156
Atwood, Amaziah, 167
Atwood, David, 155, 167
Atwood, John, 155
Atwood, Joseph, 145, 155
Atwood, Sears, 155
Atwood, Solomon, 155
Ayres, Dr. Jason, 168

Bacon, Ebenezer, 114
Bacon, Freeman, 167
Bailey, Stephen, 167
Baker, Barney, 134
Baker, Ephraim, 168
Baker, Henry, 167
Baker, Isaac, 167
Baker, John, 134
Baker, Leonard P., 168
Baker, Loren, 120
Bangs, Perez, 168
Bassett, Zenas D., 114
Baxter, Obed, 121
Berry, Howes, 120
Bowerman, Daniel, 109
Bowman, Zebulon, 109
Buck, Benjamin, 155
Butler, Capt. John, 107
Butler, Knowles, 107

Chapman, Abraham, 134
Chapman, Isaac, 134
Chapman, John, 134
Clark, Deacon Benjamin, 163
Clark, E.C., 163
Clark, Edward C., 163
Clark, George, 163

Coan, Samuel, 168
Cobb, Elkanah, 163
Cobb, Nathan F., 163
Cobb, Thomas, 163
Cole, Joshua, 163
Cole, Timothy, 163
Collins, B.H.A., 163
Collins, George, 163
Collins, George Seabury, 163
Collins, Joseph, 168
Collins, Michael, 168
Covil, Asa, 120
Crocker, Capt. John, 107
Crocker, Isaiah, 120
Crocker, Loring, 113
Crocker, Lot, 114
Crocker, Nathan, 113
Crosby, Abiel, 145
Crosby, Edmund, 145
Crosby, Edward, 145
Crosby, Hatsel, 120
Crosby, Joseph, 145
Crowell, Benjamin, 109
Crowell, Ezra, 155
Crowell, Isaiah, 119
Crowell, John, 133
Crowell, Joshua, 156
Crowell, Lewis, 119
Crowell, Nathan, 134
Crowell, Thomas, 121
Crowell, William, 133

Davis, Adrian, 109
Davis, Edmund, 109
Davis, Jabez, 109
Davis, Nymphus, 109
Davis, Russell, 119
Davis, Silas, 109
Davis, Solomon, 168
Davis, Walter, 109
Dill, Moses, 167
Dillingham Joseph, 109
Dillingham, Stephen, 109

Dimmock, John, 109
Dixon, William, 113
Doane, Herman S., 163
Doane, John, 145
Doane, Lewis, 145
Doane, Nathaniel, 155
Doane, Samuel, 155
Dunbar, Benjamin, 156

Eldred, Nathaniel, 109
Eldredge, Truman D., 113
Eldridge, Elra, 155
Eldridge, Ephraim, 109
Eldridge, Jonathan, 156
Eldridge, Reuben, 155
Eldridge, Thomas, 146
Engals, James, 145

Freeman, Barnabas, 163
Freeman, Josiah, 145
Freeman, Simeon, 114

Gage, Zenas, 114
Gifford, Edward, 120
Gifford, James, 109
Gifford, Prince, 120
Gifford, Silas, 109
Gifford, Theophilus, 109
Gifford, William, 109
Goodspeed, Seth, 113
Gorham, Henry, 155
Gorham, Nathaniel, 113
Gould, Nathaniel, 146
Gould, Thomas, 146
Gross, Hinks, 168
Grozier, John, 168

Hamblen, Cornelius, 167
Hall, Daniel, 134
Hallett, Henry, 114
Hallett, Joshua, 114
Hallett, Warren, 114
Hamilton, William, 155
Harding, Elisha, 155
Harding, Isaiah, 155

Harding, Joseph, 155
Harding, Prince, 156
Hardy, Isaac, 155
Hatch, Davis, 107
Hatch, John, 107
Higgins, Daniel, 145
Higgins, Eliahim, 146
Higgins, Joshua, 163
Higgins, Thomas, 146
Hinckley, Allen, 168
Hinckley, Benjamin, 168
Hinckley, David, 114
Hinckley, George, 113
Hinckley, Warren, 114
Holbrook, Joseph, 167
Hopkins, Asa, 145
Hopkins, Elisha, 145
Hopkins, Henry L., 113
Hopkins, Isaac, 145
Hopkins, Josiah, 145
Hopkins, Michael, 168
Hopkins, Thomas, 168
Horton, Sparrow, 145
Howes, Alvin, 113
Howes, David, 134
Howes, Eli, 134
Howes, Enoch, 155
Howes, Micajah, 155
Howes, Lothrop, 134
Howes, Thomas, 156
Howes, William, 134
Hurd, Joseph, 145

Jarvis, Edward, 145
Jenkins, Capt. Weston, 107
Jones, Capt. Silas, 107

Kelley, David, 120
Kelley, Seth, 119
Kelley, Zeno, 119
Kemp, Wells, E., 167
Kendrick, Edward, 155
Kendrick, Henry, 146
Kendrick, Josiah, 156
Kennedy, John, 168

Kenrick, John, 146
Knowles, Captain Nathaniel, 145
Knowles, Harding, 163
Knowles, Isaac, 145
Knowles, Joshua, 163
Knowles, Major Henry, 145
Knowles, Samuel, 163
Knowles, Seth, 145
Knowles, William, 163

Lawrence, Silas, 107
Lawrence, Thomas, 107
Lewis, Elnathan, 114
Lewis, Isaiah, 155
Linnell, Elkanah, 145
Lombard, David, 168
Lombard, Lewis, 168
Loveland, Joseph, 155
Loveland, Timothy, 156
Lovell, A.W., 114
Lovell, George, 113
Lovell, Gorham, 114
Lovell, Henry, 113
Lovell, Jacob, 113

Marchant, Freeman, 114
Marchant, Deacon James, 114
Mayo, Barnabas, 163
Mayo, Thomas, 146
Myrick, William, 145, 146

Newcomb, Elisha, 168
Nickerson, Allen, 156
Nickerson, Caleb, 156
Nickerson, Ensign, Jr., 156
Nickerson, Ensign, Sr., 155
Nickerson, Jesse, 156
Nickerson, Joshua, 155
Nickerson, Myrick, 156
Nickerson, Nathaniel, 145
Nickerson, Orick, 156
Nickerson, Richard, 156
Nickerson, Salathiel, 156
Nickerson, Samuel, 156
Nickerson, Zenas, 155

Nye, Sylvanus, 168

Otis, Amos, 113

Paddock, Enoch, 134
Paddock, Judah, 134
Paine, Capt. Elisha, 168
Paine, Joshua, 163
Paine, Seth, 163
Paine, Solomon, 168
Parker, John, 109
Parker, Ward M., 109

Rich, Doane, 168
Rich, Ephraim D., 168
Rich, Nehemiah, 168
Rogers, Adna, 146
Rogers, Asa, 146
Rogers, Blossom, 145
Rogers, Sears, 145
Ryder, Christopher, 155
Ryder, Isaiah, 155
Ryder, James, 156
Ryder, John, 156
Ryder, Kimball, Sr., 155
Ryder, Kimball, Jr., 155
Ryder, Reuben, 155
Ryder, Samuel, 168

Sanford, Ephraim, 107, 109
Scudder, Deacon, 113
Scudder, Ebenezer, 113
Scudder, Frederick, 114
Seabury, Isaac, 145
Seabury, Joseph, 145
Sears, Barnabas, 120
Sears, Barnabas H., 134
Sears, Capt. John, 133, 134
Sears, Daniel, 134
Sears, Edmund, 122
Sears, Edward, 134
Sears, Elkanah, Jr., 134
Sears, Elkahan, Sr., 134
Sears, Ezra, 134
Sears, Jacob, 134

Sears, Joseph, 134
Sears, Joshua, 134
Sears, Major John, 134
Sears, Nathan, 134
Sears, Richard, 156
Sears, Thomas, 134
Sears, William, 134
Sherman, Abraham, 119
Shiverick, Asa, 134
Sloane, Joseph G., 145
Small, Colonel Joshua, 168
Smith, Capt. William, 145
Smith, David, 120, 168
Smith, John, 168
Smith, Samuel, 167
Smith, Seth, 145
Smith, Stephen, 119, 155
Smith, Thomas, 155
Snow, Alvin, 114
Snow, Gideon S., 145
Snow, Jesse, 145, 168
Snow, Michael, 168
Snow, Major Joel, 163
Snow, Nathaniel, 155
Snow, Reuben, 156, 168
Snow, Samuel, 163
Snow, Shubel, 168
Sparrow, Josiah, 145
Stevens, Jonah, 168
Stevens, Levi, 168
Sturgis, Mrs, 113
Swift, Daniel, 109
Swift, Capt. Elijah, 107
Swift, Joseph, 109
Swift, Moses, 109
Swift, Seth, 109
Swift, Silas, 109

Taylor, Christopher, 155
Taylor, Collins, 155
Taylor, John, 156
Taylor, Joseph, 156
Taylor, Samuel, 155
Taylor, Zenas, 156
Taylor, Zoeth, 145

Tucker, Lothrup, 113

Walker, Benjamin, 163
Walker, Peter, 163
Whorf, Jonathan, 168
Wicks, George W., 109
Wicks, Marcus, 109
Wing, Daniel, 119
Wing, George, 119
Wing, Robert, 119, 120
Winslow, Abraham, 134
Winslow, Isaac, 134
Winslow, Kenelm, 134
Winslow, Nathaniel, 134
Witherell, Benjamin, 167
Whitman, Deacon, 167
Whitman, Samuel, 113
Wood, Francis, 120

Young, Asa, 113
Young, Captain, 156
Young, Johah, 155
Young, Jonathan, 145
Young, Joseph, 155, 156
Young, Rufus, 156
Young, Samuel, H., 156

LIST OF ILLUSTRATIONS

Acorn, illustration, 84

Barnstable Harbor - aerial view, 115
Barnstable County Court House, 49
Barnstable Meeting House, 10
Bass River, 126, 127
Bass River - illustration, 128
Billingsgate Island, 202
Billingsgate Island Lighthouse, 202
Blacksmith's Shop, Orleans, 88

Cannon - 1812, 49
Cape Cod, 198
Captain Linnell House, 43
Chancellor Livingston, 40
Chatham - aerial photograph, 159
Chatham - 1831 map, 158
Chatham - 1851 map, 161
Chatham Stage, 70
Coastal schooners, 36
Cora M., 157
Cranberry harvest, Yarmouth, 88
Crocker, Loring - saltworks, 112
Cutting Ice, Yarmouth, 86

D.A. Small, Whaling Brig, 60
Dexter Grist Mill, 82
Doane, Isiah - Deed, 101
Drummer, 86

Early Homestead, viii, 153
Eastham - 1851 map, 162, 165
East Mill, Orleans, 146
Eastham Windmill, 164

Falmouth Center - map, 106
Farris Windmill, 78
Fishing vessel, 34

Grecian, 157

Harbor illustration, 44
Harwich Powder House, 48
Hattie, 126
Highland Light - RR engine, 196
Highland Light House, 58
Hyannis - map, 117

Jonathan Young Windmill, 76
Judah Baker Windmill, 78

Knowles, Freeman - Deed, 99
Kutusoff, whaleship, 75

Lafayette salts, 4
Lifesaving illustration, 180
Longfellow, 198

Nobscusset House, Dennis, 91

Old Colony No. 186, RR engine, 196
Orleans - 1831 map, 147
Orleans - 1848 map, 150
Orleans - 1851 map, 148
Orleans Packet ship, 66
Orleans Town Cove - map, 103
Orleans train, 195
Osterville - map, 116

Packet vessel advertisements, 68
Packet vessel illustration, 64
Pants Factory, Orleans, 89
Pants Factory workers, 90
Plymouth Rock wreck, 56
Provincetown - 1837 map, 172, 173
Provincetown harbor view, 178
Provincetown 1840 illustration, 184
Provincetown Town Hall, 170
Provincetown train, 200
Provincetown waterfront, 170

Quamquisset Harbor - map, 108
Quivet Neck - map, 24
Quivet Neck - aerial photos, 25, 132

Railroad advertisments, 194
Red Sea Balsam team, 144
Rock Harbor - aerial photo, 149
Rock Harbor Historic Marker, 48

Saltmills, 21, 111, 125, 154
Saltworks, abandoned, 182
Saltworks boards, 138, 139
Saltworks, Bourne, 184
Saltworks, illustration, 28, 72
Saltworks, Chatham, 29
Saltworks, model, 159
Saltworks, Orleans, 151
Saltworks, Quivet Neck, 14, 133
Saltworks, South Yarmouth, 3, 11, 18,
          120, 124
Saltworks, West Brewster, iv, 143
Saltworks, Yarmouthport, 131
Sandwich Center - map, 104
Sandwich Glass Works, 5, 84

Schooner underway, 46, 175
Schooner illustration, 152
Sears Monument, 20
Shipwreck, 56
Shiverick Shipyard plaque, 92
Somerset wreck, 16
South Yarmouth - map, 122
South Yarmouth - aerial view, 123
Stoney Brook Grist Mill, 82
Styles, womens, 144

Truro - 1848 map, 169
Truro Shipwreck Memorial Tablet, 54

Wellfleet - 1850 map, 166
West Brewster - map, 142
West Falmouth - map, 110
West Yarmouth - map, 118
Whaling illustration, 74
Windmill illustration, 81

Yarmouthport barn, 129
Yarmouthport, Main St., 131
Yarmouthport - map, 130

ENOCH HARDING'S SALTWORKS

On the next four pages are drawings of Enoch Harding's saltworks in Chatham as they appeared, circa 1830. The plans were rendered by the Works Progress Administration back in the 1930's when the country was in a depression. The scale drawings seem to be accurate except for possibly one error found in the title. The list of Chatham assessments on page 160 does not list Enoch Harding as an owner. The names on the list include Isaiah Harding and following him, Enoch Howes. The names may have been entered wrong on the tax list or, when reading the list, the architect may have juxtapositioned the two first names. It is quite evident that, over a period of one hundred and sixty years, the accuracy in these listings did not command a high priority.

The plot plan on drawing number one shows the location of the saltworks in South Chatham at Buck's Creek on Nantucket Sound. Drawing number two contains information on the elevations used in construction of the saltworks. The third drawing outlines details of the vats and drawing number four features the plans for a salt mill. The notes on the plans indicate that: "water was only drawn for vats on incoming tides to get as high a salt content as possible." Another note on the plans stated: "These works were located when possible on sand beaches. The sand intensifying the heat of the sun by reflection which expedited the evaporation of the brine. Vats were located true north and south - covers sliding to the north."

The discovery of these plans was a bonus while searching for other material at the Cape Cod National Seashore library at the headquarters building in Wellfleet. I am indebted to Frank Ackerman, Chief of the Interpretive Division at the Seashore for his assistance in the acquisition of this material.

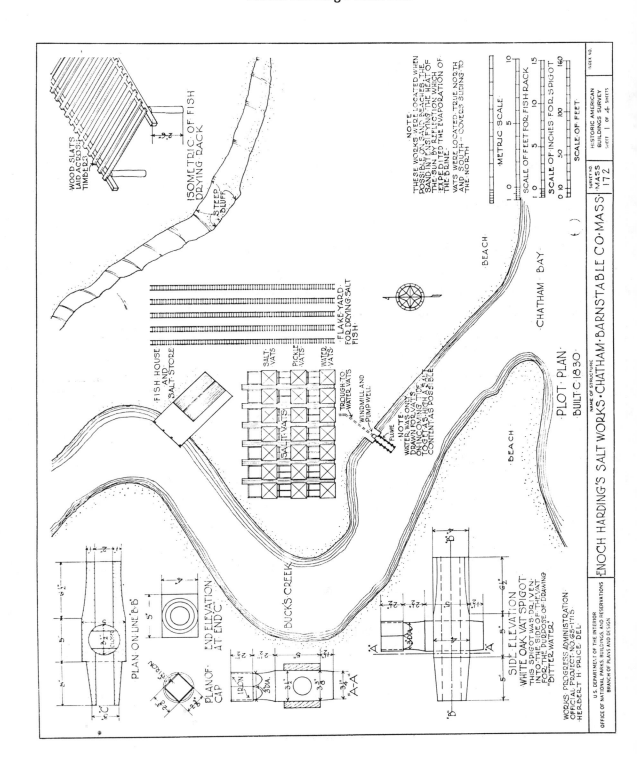

ISOMETRIC OF FISH DRYING RACK

WOOD SLATS LAID ACROSS TIMBERS

STEEP BLUFF

FLAKE YARD FOR DRYING FISH

FISH HOUSE AND SALT STORE

SALT VATS
PICKLE VATS
WATER VATS

SALT VATS

TROUGH TO WATER VATS

WINDMILL AND PUMP WELL

FLUME

NOTE
WATER WAS ONLY DRAWN FOR VATS ON INCOMING TIDE TOGET AS HIGH A SALT CONTENT AS POSSIBLE

BUCK'S CREEK

BEACH

CHATHAM BAY

BEACH

NOTE
THESE WORKS WERE LOCATED WHEN POSSIBLE ON SAND BEACHES THE SAND INTENSIFYING THE HEAT OF THE SUN BY REFLECTION WHICH EXPEDITED THE EVAPORATION OF THE BRINE.
VATS WERE LOCATED TRUE NORTH AND SOUTH — COVERS SLIDING TO THE NORTH.

METRIC SCALE

SCALE OF FEET FOR FISH RACK

SCALE OF INCHES FOR SPIGOT

SCALE OF FEET

PLAN ON LINE B·B

END ELEVATION AT END C

PLAN OF CAP

PLAN OF APRON

A·A

SIDE ELEVATION
WHITE OAK VAT SPIGOT
THIS SPIGOT WAS DRIVEN INTO THE SIDE OF THE VAT FOR THE PURPOSE OF DRAWING "BITTER WATER"

PLOT·PLAN
BUILT C·1830

WORKS PROGRESS ADMINISTRATION
OFFICIAL PROJECT NO.65-1715
HERBERT H. PRICE. DEL.

U.S. DEPARTMENT OF THE INTERIOR
OFFICE OF NATIONAL PARKS, BUILDINGS, AND RESERVATIONS
BRANCH OF PLANS AND DESIGN

NAME OF STRUCTURE
ENOCH HARDING'S SALT WORKS·CHATHAM·BARNSTABLE CO·MASS

HISTORIC AMERICAN BUILDINGS SURVEY
SHEET 1 OF 4 SHEETS

SURVEY NO
MASS
172

INDEX NO.

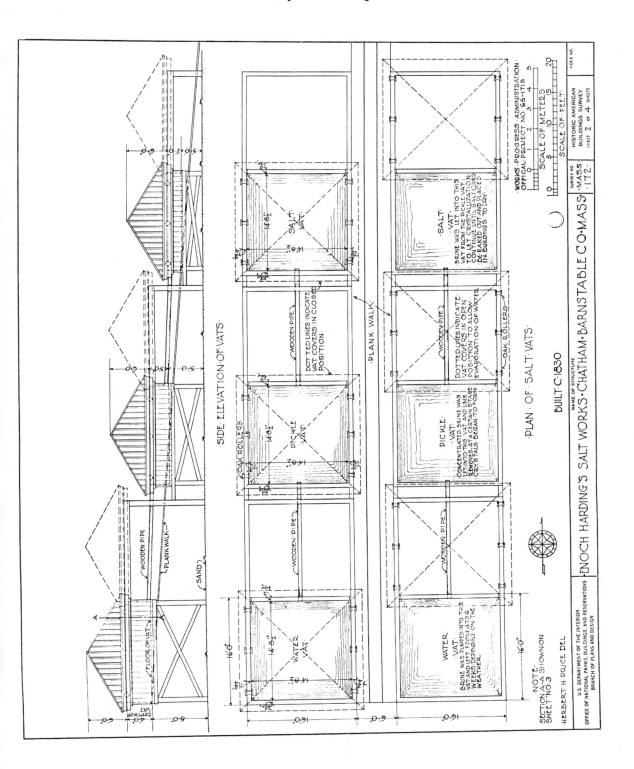

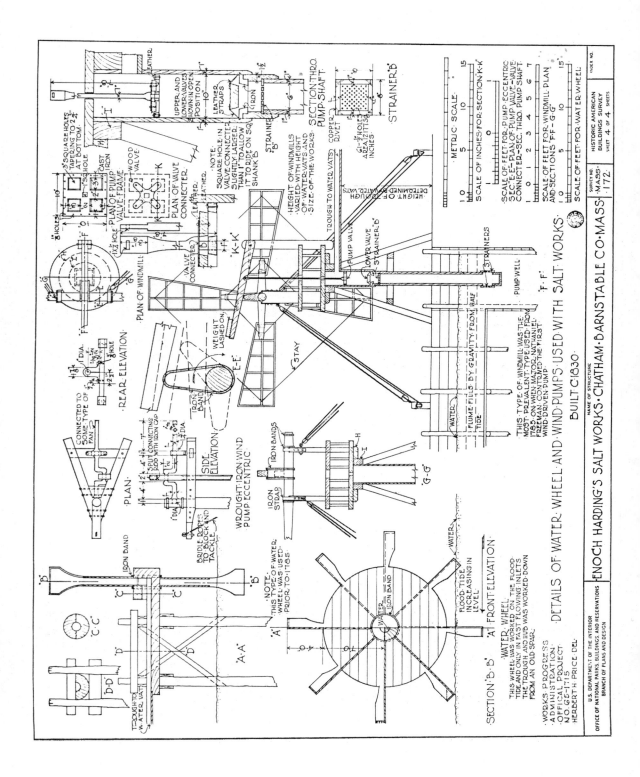

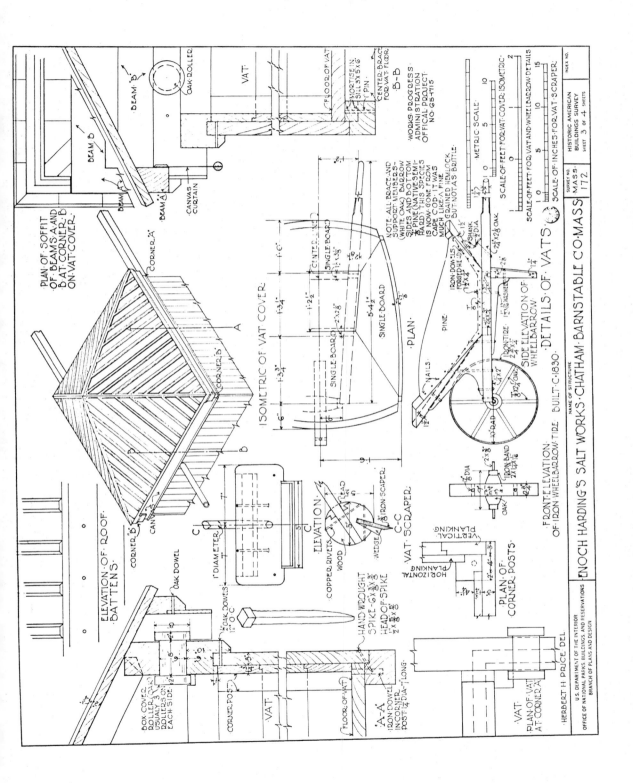

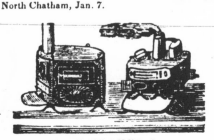

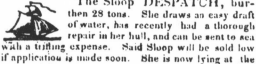